the boy's book of
Outdoor Discovery

OTHER BOOKS BY THE AUTHOR:

Campfire and Council Ring Programs
Campfire Adventure Stories
Indian Adventure Trails
Living Like Indians
American Indian Legends
Book of American Indian Games
Treasury of Memory-Making Campfires
New Games for 'Tween-Agers
More New Games for 'Tween-Agers
Fun With Brand-New Games
Games from Bible Lands and Times
Knotcraft
ABC's of Camping
The Boy's Book of Backyard Camping
The Boy's Book of Hiking
The Boy's Book of Biking
The Boy's Book of Rainy-Day Doings
The Boy's Book of Indian Skills

the boy's book of
Outdoor
Discovery
Allan A. Macfarlan

GALAHAD BOOKS • NEW YORK CITY

Published by Galahad Books, a division of A & W Pro-
motional Book Corporation, 95 Madison Avenue, New
York, N.Y. 10016, by arrangement with Stackpole Books,
Cameron and Kelker Streets, Harrisburg, Pa. 17105.

Library of Congress Catalog Card No. 73-81645
ISBN: 0-88365-029-0

Manufactured in the United States of America.

Contents

CHAPTER 1

Skills
For The
Outdoors

WONDER AND CURIOSITY are closely linked to discovery. What's that? What's over there? What's in there? Where does that path lead? are all simple questions which have triggered exploration at home and the world over.

Heading for Discovery

Though unexplored country may be far away, a lot of discoveries may be made in cities where there are parks, play areas, ponds, lakes, and public wooded lots. Some of these may be found in and around urban and suburban developments as well as in the country. Even in a small park there is always a great deal happening in the world of nature, most of it unnoticed by the casual visitor. Corner lots, parks, and fields too may have their own nature shows in action, but one must learn to observe, not just take a quick look, in order to really see what is going on.

Boys who live in big cities can usually go fairly far afield, without spending much money, by using one of the many public transportation systems which link cities, towns, and suburban areas with the great outdoors. Even though a fellow may be able to do a lot of outdoor discovery alone, it is even better when he takes a fellow explorer, with more or less the same interests, along.

Using one's eyes to the best advantage is often the secret of worthwhile discovery. Asking the questions Where? What? When? and Why? is a good way to become a keen outdoor detective.

Following are some pointers which will help outdoor adventurers find their way, attract rescuers if they become lost, keep track of the time, judge what the weather will be like, and carry loads comfortably.

Pathfinding

Indian scouts and guides rarely lost their way. Most of them wisely guessed that they had no built-in sense of direction. This is something that only a few outdoors people realize today. Anyone who believes that he has a natural "sense of direction" should make the following test, then forget about his former belief.

SENSE-OF-DIRECTION TEST Make the test on smooth ground, such as a field in a park, where one can walk for at least fifty yards without having obstacles in the way. Have someone place a white handkerchief or other visible object on the ground fifty long paces away. Then, with an effective blindfold covering both eyes, try to walk at a normal pace in a straight line to the handkerchief. If luck holds on the first try, make two more blindfolded attempts, to decide just what built-in sense of direction you really have. Many experienced outdoors people err by as much as fifty yards in this test, based on a 100-yard walk.

Finding the way in unknown country is not always easy. It is best to expect some difficulties and keep a sharp lookout for landmarks, the position of the sun, and the length of time spent In walking in a certain direction, so that on the way back one does not need to guess the way out. Nobody likes to admit that he is lost. Even Daniel Boone never admitted that he had been lost, but he did confess that he had been "mixed up a bit" for several days at a time.

MAP AND COMPASS   Taking along a big-scale map and a reliable compass is the surest way to avoid becoming lost in unknown country. With a little practice a hiker will be able to use a compass well and understand a map. He will know that north is at the top of the map, be able to recognize the various signs on the map, and by looking at the scale will be able to tell just how much a mile covers on the map. It is easy to buy a good map and compass. They cost little and give a lot of protection against getting lost. But if you should get lost sometime, the following are ways to get found.

THINK WAY   The first thing to do is to keep calm. Remember that nearly all people are found these days, before being lost for long. Searchers, fire warden lookouts, and low-flying planes are likely to spot any help signals. Some of these are given below under SOS Signals.

Try to think clearly at which point you became aware that familiar country and landmarks were no longer visible. If there is a high recognizable peak in the surrounding country, head for it. Or there may be a river or other unmistakable landmark to which you know the general direction. Without some idea about such possible directional helps, better stay put, signal, and let the searchers find you. This is especially true if it is late in the day, even though you may have to overnight where you are or nearby. A change of position might be made necessary, however, by the need to find water, firewood, or a less exposed spot in which to pass the night.

SUN WAY   So long as it is sunny and you know what lies in a certain direction—whether it be north, south, east, or west— and the approximate distance to that point, you are not really lost. Use the sun as a compass, knowing that it rises in the east and sets in the west. Facing east, north is to the left, south to the right, and west behind you.

STAR WAY   The easiest star guide, used by the Indians and called by them "the-star-that-does-not-move," is the North Star. In fair weather the Big Dipper may be easily recognized among the other constellations and stars. Use the two stars which form the front of the dipper as "pointers," and they will indicate the bright North Star, which always shines in the north.

Despite this, it is wiser not to try to travel in any direction across country after dark. There are too many hazards. Wait for the morning's sun and give the searchers a chance to locate you.

BACKTRACKING   On a hike in wooded country, when one intends to return by the same route, pathfinding is developed by keeping an eye on the position of the sun, when starting out and returning. It is a good idea to note prominent landmarks on the way to the destination, and frequently look back to be able to know what the trail back looks like, because the appearance of a trail when backtracking is entirely different.

Strangely formed trees, striking outcroppings of rock, an old shack or barn, and similar landmarks will act as guides to direct you back to the starting point of an outdoor discovery jaunt. Of course, with a compass, backtracking is very easy.

TELLING DIRECTION BY WATCH   Here's a handy way for those without a compass to use a watch instead. Point the hour hand at the sun, as you hold the watch flat, face up, in your hand or on a flat surface. Halfway between the hour hand and the 12 lies south, so north will be in the opposite direction, as illustrated. This method provides fairly accurate direction-finding between six in the morning and six in the evening. For localities where daylight saving time is in force, use the 1 instead of the 12.

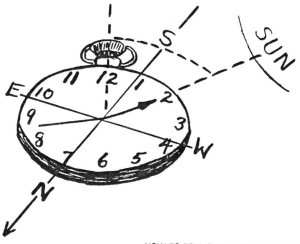

SOS Signals

When a person who is lost wishes to attract the attention of possible rescuers, he uses the following signals:

On a clearing or open ground, where he and his signals may be seen, he lays out the letters "SOS" on the ground, using white stones or pieces of silver birch logs if there are any on the ground in that area. White cloth (which a lost person is not likely to have with him) can be used to make a part of the signal. This signal is the most difficult to give, since the letters should be very large in order to be seen from the air.

All nearly universal distress signals are given in various ways by a series of threes:

- three fires lit in a line or in the form of a triangle.
- three smoke signals from three fires covered with green grass or leaves.
- anything that will send up three columns of smoke.
- whistles in groups of three.
- bangs on a hollow tree, in groups of three.

- flashes from a signal mirror or ordinary mirror, in groups of three.

Making a Sun Clock

Learning to estimate the time fairly accurately by the position of one's shadow takes quite a lot of practice, and noon is about the only time that a beginner can tell with any certainty. Some African tribes describe noon as "the time when the chicken sits on her shadow." Instead of trying to estimate sun time by the length of your shadow, at different times of day, it is easier to make a shadow clock, which is really a sundial. A shadow clock outdoors takes up quite a lot of room, around 12 feet square, and unless it is built on a private piece of ground, passers-by may help themselves to the long, straight pole which is required and the pegs which are driven into the ground to mark the hours. Here is a sun clock that is portable, is easy to make, and takes up little room.

Use a piece of board 16 inches square and 1/2 inch or 3/4 inch thick. Sandpaper it smooth, then mark a 15-inch circle on it. Divide the circle into 24 equal parts; then mark the numbers, as in the illustration. These numbers can be marked with India ink or indelible pencil. They represent the hours. Those on the left side are the morning hours, to noon, and the ones at the right are the afternoon hours, to sunset. No numbers are required on the lower part of the board, since

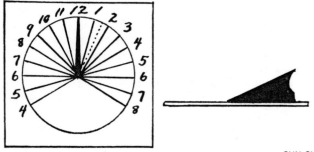

SUN CLOCK
Left: clock face. *Right:* side view of indicator

it represents the hours of darkness. The thick center line appearing in the drawing shows where the indicator, marking the shadow time, is glued to the board. This pointer should be at about a 35-degree angle to the base, as shown in the drawing. The dotted line between the 1 and the 2 shows how the shadow of the pointer indicates the time.

To use the sun clock on a sunny day, lay it on some smooth, flat surface outdoors on the ground or on a flat roof, with the clock pointer facing north. Merely estimating the position of the sun will not assure correct time. The easiest way to set the sun clock is with a compass. Place the clock so that the pointer, aligned with the compass needle, faces north.

Weather Lore

Being able to know what the weather is going to do is very important for outdoor people, whether they are going hiking, fishing, kite-flying, or boating. Unfortunately, in spite of huge amounts spent on scientific instruments for weather stations, many outdoorsmen are still forced to trust to their own interpretations of nature's weather signs, rather than accept the radio and television "weather forecasts."

Whether it rains or shines is going to make a big difference to those going on a picnic, but the question is which to expect before starting out. It helps to remember what people used to say about weather signs because some of these old maxims were, and still are, fairly accurate. For instance:

- A red sky at night is the sailor's delight.
- The evening gray, the morning red, will pour down rain upon your head.
- When the wind's before the rain, soon you may make sail again.
- A rainbow in the morning (forming in the west) is the sailor's warning.

Many Indians could make weather forecasts which were quite as accurate or more so than many of the science-based predictions of today's weathermen. These old Indians had learned and developed their skills by keen observation of nature in general. When the wind blew from a certain direction, birds and animals acted strangely, and strange, faint noises were heard, or odors were more noticeable than usual, these weather-wise old men were able to tell a party of braves leaving on a hunt or fishing trip just what sort of weather they would have for at least the next few days. By similar signs these weather-lore masters were able to tell fishermen whether they would have good catches or not, and whether it was safe to set out on a canoe voyage of several days on a great lake. These weather prophets knew when rain or cold weather was on its way, or even whether it would rain before morning, and their forecasts were nearly always exact. What sort of help did these forecasters get from Mother Nature?

Here are some of the signs which influenced these old men's weather predictions and which still hold true today.

FAIR WEATHER SIGNS
- Sky colors foretell the weather for a day or two. An evening sky that is rose or red means fair weather for the next day.
- A "mackerel" sky (which looks a little like fish scales) usually means fair weather, though it might also bring a few showers.
- When the smoke from a campfire rises straight up, good weather will continue.
- When insect-eating birds fly high, the weather will remain fair.
- When the grass is wet with dew on a summer night, the next day will be fair.
- A rainbow in the evening sky predicts that the next morning will be fair.
- When a few bright stars are visible in a pale sky, good weather will continue.

BAD WEATHER SIGNS
- A pale yellow sky at sunset generally foretells a rainy day ahead.
- A dull copper-red sky in the east, shortly before sunup, indicates rain.

- A grayish-blue sky, dotted with small gray-black clouds, tells of rain soon.
- A morning rainbow in the west predicts rain on the way.
- When the moon wears a halo, especially when the halo is some distance from the moon, rain is on its way.
- When crows roll and perform acrobatics in the air, high winds are near.
- When a rainy forenoon does not clear before one o'clock, the rain is likely to continue until evening, at least.
- When atmospheric pressure keeps campfire smoke from rising straight up, rain is not far off.
- Distant objects appear closer and clearer when rain is not far away.
- Field sparrows often splash in old rain puddles when rain is not far away.
- Odors, pleasant or bad, become more noticeable shortly before rain.

WINDS FOR THE FISHERMAN There are generally accepted theories about good and bad winds for fishing. Sometimes these theories are upset by a local fisherman who has learned by experience about the effects of winds on fishing in a certain locality. So it is wise to ask a local fisherman who knows what weather is to be expected in his area and its effect on fishing.

General beliefs about fishing weather are:

- Wind from the south means good fishing.
- Wind from the west is often favorable for fishing.
- Winds from the east and north often mean poor fishing.

The Knack of Handling Loads

Almost since the beginning of time, man has sought the best ways to lift, move, and carry things. The cavemen had to find a way to roll huge boulders in front of the entrances to their caves, in order to keep cave bears and sabre-toothed cats out. The Indians of the Northwest Coast learned to move huge canoes, and much earlier, the Egyptians became expert in everything concerning the arts of lifting, moving, and logistics. Knowing how to do difficult things the easy way is one of the things boys should learn in order to make things easier for themselves outdoors. Here are some easy ways of lifting heavy things with the least strain and effort.

HOW TO LIFT HEAVY THINGS SAFELY The act of lifting affects not only the muscles of the body but also the eyes. Lifting too heavy a weight can cause serious injury even to a strong man. Because of this, great care should be taken when lifting anything.

To lift any weight safely and easily, one must first of all lift in a relaxed position. The knees should be bent slightly at the start of a lift and the arms and back used in a way which lets the strain be taken gradually and smoothly. The straightening-up process, when lifting a heavy weight or even a lighter one, should be slow and without jerking.

DUAL LIFTING It is much safer and easier to have another fellow give a hand when a heavy object has to be lifted or moved than to play the dangerous game of strong man and try to tackle the load alone.

Timing is important when two are lifting a heavy object. The even distribution of weight can be assured by one lifter (decided on in advance) saying slowly, "Ready—lift."

Even greater care is necessary when two people are lowering a heavy object to the ground. One of the two bearers is chosen to place his end of the load on the ground first. When the object is an inch or so above ground level, he slips his fingers out from under his end of the load so it lands smoothly. The other bearer then releases his hold without the risk of the first bearer's fingers being crushed.

MOVING HEAVY THINGS When only a short distance has to be covered, a heavy object is usually moved from one place to another by pulling or pushing it. Whether one should pull or shove is decided by the ease with which the object moves in response to one of these two methods.

THE INDIAN SLIDE METHOD Some Indian tribes discovered that a simple way to move heavy objects from place to place over fairly smooth, level ground was to load the things onto a piece of blanket, cloth, or animal hide large enough to allow the objects to be pulled quite easily. This method worked especially well on grass or through forest clearings carpeted with pine needles.

This simple slide method works equally well at home, when moving a heavy trunk or other object on a short length of strong cloth or small rug over a wooden floor.

POLE CARRIES The best and easiest way to carry loads smoothly is to have two bearers walk or march out of step. That is how stretcher bearers carry a stretcher so that the patient is carried smoothly.

Laborers in various countries carry loads—sometimes very heavy ones—slung from the center of two strong, lightweight poles which are carried on two bearers' shoulders. Sometimes the load is suspended at about waist level from one pole carried on one shoulder of each bearer.

This carry is also useful to tote short lengths of not too heavy logs. A log is slung from beneath the pole, as illustrated, with

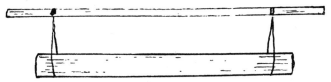

POLE CARRY FOR TOTING A LOG

the ends of the long pole resting on the left or right shoulder of each of the two bearers.

STICK CARRIES Many people carry things on sticks not only for convenience but also because the bundles on sticks are easier to carry. Gypsies, tramps, and the swagmen of Australia, for instance, often carry bundles of various sorts tied to the end of a stick, the stick being carried over the shoulder and supported by one hand. Changing the position of the stick changes the pressure on the shoulder.

Bundles are made lighter by dual carries. Whatever has to be carried is tied to the middle of a stout stick about six feet long and the two carriers walk side by side with the bundle slung between them. On narrow roads and paths, one carrier walks ahead of the other.

HEAD CARRIES   Carrying loads on top of the head is common all over the world. Some errand boys carry baskets on top of a small ring of twisted cloth worn on top of the head. The ring helps keep the basket balanced on the head. Sometimes a camper or hiker is seen carrying a heavy load in this manner. Such a change, at times, rests his back and shoulders.

BACK CARRIES   There are actually few back carries in which the back supports the weight, except when one carries another person on his back, though sometimes, especially in the Orient, one sees men and women carry heavy loads on their bent backs. They become so bent, over the years, that even without a load they cannot stand upright. When carrying a heavy pack, the greatest weight of the load rests on the shoulders of the pack carrier, especially when he walks in the approved upright position.

SHOULDER CARRIES   People all over the world carry loads of various sorts on one or sometimes two shoulders. Usually a log or bundle is carried on one shoulder, or a camper or sailor carries a duffle bag on one shoulder. Balancing things properly, especially things such as long poles or planks carried on the shoulders, is a very important part of transporting objects easily. When the right balance is arrived at, by the trial-and-error method, much of the weight of the objects carried seems to be taken care of by balance.

In a shoulder carry, the strain is relieved by changing the load from shoulder to shoulder, as one shoulder becomes tired.

In some parts of the world, a really heavy load which is pliant is bent into the form of a horse collar, the center placed around the back of the neck, and one end balanced on each shoulder.

Usually the closest that most campers or hikers come to the shoulder carry is carrying blankets, tent sections, or ground sheets, tied in the form of a horse collar and slung over one shoulder and over the chest. Sometimes such bandoliers, as they are sometimes called, are quite heavy because the bearer has wrapped some pieces of pliable camping gear into the center of the roll.

LOGROLLING This may be done on a small scale by using a strong, straight pole or crowbar if one is handy. The easiest way to roll logs over fairly smooth ground, free from stumps, is illustrated. All that is needed is a strong peg and a length of

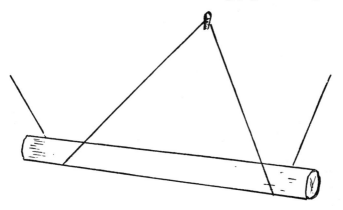

HOW TO ROLL A LOG

rope. Almost everywhere, these days, conservation forbids cutting down live trees for logs. This does not prevent the outdoors boy from using down (dead) logs for building outdoor things, such as rafts. Sound, down logs float much more easily than freshly cut logs, anyway.

ROCK DISPOSAL Here is the best way to get rid of a few rocks and boulders which may litter a piece of flat, useful ground. Dig holes directly beside the rocks, topple them into the holes with a pole lever, and fill in the hollows with the loose earth dug from the holes. Tread down this earth.

CHAPTER 2

Discovering
Nature's
Magic

THERE IS MUCH of mystery and magic going on every hour of the day in nature's wonderful workshop. The American Indians got very close to some of these marvels, though they had neither microscope nor science on which to base their studies. They simply looked closely, thought about what they saw, and discussed the things which they found most remarkable with friends. Today, though our outdoors is much more limited than theirs and our study may have to be done in a park, field, limited stretch of woodland, or corner lot, there is still much to see and wonder at. Take a bus to the end of the line and stroll along the banks or shores of a pond, lake, river, or stream, and observe as much as possible, making notes and drawings of interesting things you see. A few sketches, of leaves or flowers, even if they are rough-and-ready ones, can be identified at home, later.

For those who combine outdoor discovery with indoor discovery, the fascinating world of nature will wear a new look, and they will no longer be a stranger at its borders. There are many fine, easy to read and understand books on nature in public libraries. Much information may also be found in inexpensive paperbacks. A fellow should think of the things in the vast outdoors which interest him most. These subjects may be listed under such headings as natural history, birds, animals, ponds, insects, amphibians, reptiles, aquatic life, and geology. The best and most useful of these books are usually well illustrated, adding to their interest and the reader's knowledge. Reading books of this sort usually leads to the exploration of a natural history museum where the birds, animals, insects, and other things read about seem to come to life. The descriptive cards on various cases will confirm and probably add to previously acquired knowledge.

Window Gardens

One of the best ways to learn about plants is to grow them in a window garden. A window garden can be a window box, a few flowerpots, small wooden boxes, or tin cans filled with plants and/or flowers. By outfoxing balky plants, so that they want to grow, and by outwitting weather conditions, a fellow can become a gardener, of sorts. Whether he becomes a master gardener with a "green thumb" depends a great deal on the amount of experimenting he does and how much patience he has. A lot can be learned by reading a few paperbacks which tell about flowers, wild flowers, and foliage plants, which do not flower, but are usually easier to grow than many flowering plants. Most important, a window gardener has the fun and wonder of seeing nature at work.

CHOOSING THE BEST EXPOSURE   The direction in which a window box faces will decide what can be grown in it easily. Sunlight, light, and heat determine this. Most wild or cultivated flowering plants need sunlight, while foliage plants get along well with light alone. This means choosing the right plants for the exposure a windowsill provides. A window facing south, east, or west, is fine for most plants, though some of the hardier ones will adapt themselves to a northern exposure. For instance, geraniums glory in direct sunlight, while wax begonias manage to get along, though not happily, with almost no sunlight.

TRAYS Trays are most useful for window gardens. They can be bought cheaply in garden supply stores and some ten cent stores. These trays come in various sizes, from 6 inches to 3 feet in length, and are made of metal such as zinc or of pottery. They range from 3 to 6 inches in width and are from 1 to 3 inches deep. The foot of the tray should be covered with small, pretty pebbles which can be bought cheaply or gathered on a pebble-gathering expedition.

FLOWERPOTS AND BOXES The flowerpots, tin cans, metal boxes, small homemade wooden boxes, or ones given away by food stores need a few small holes punched in the foot of each before being placed on the pebbles in the tray. Little pottery, terra cotta, or plastic containers can be bought for a few cents, but it is more interesting to improvise. One can easily build a box of the size required to fit loosely into the tray, which takes care of drainage through small holes bored in the foot of the box. These boxes may be made from pine or other softwood boards about half an inch thick or from orange crate slats, held together with screws or thin nails about 1 inch long.

Apartment dwellers should keep in mind the neighbors who live in apartments below, and also the people on the sidewalk below, if they decide to fasten brackets or struts onto narrow windowsills in order to make them wider. Unless a really good job is done, there is always the danger of a tray or pot falling overboard and injuring someone underneath.

MAKING A TRELLIS One has to be ready for the quick growth of most vines and prepare some form of trellis to support them. A trellis can be made by tying together thin strips or rods of wood or plastic, or by stringing cords or lengths of thin picture wire across the window frame and fastening them on each side with small tacks or staples.

WINDOW GARDEN WITH TRELLIS

GENERAL POINTERS   Thousands of books and articles have been written about growing all sorts of flowers and plants in all sorts of window gardens and boxes, both inside and outside the windows. Most stores which sell flowers, plants, and seeds have salesmen who are glad to give good advice regarding special problems. A few general pointers and ideas will help you to get started, though.

You can buy bags of earth for very little money. Fill cans, pots, or boxes loosely with this earth and plant the seed or seeds in them. Your florist, seed store, or often ten cent stores, will supply information on what seeds or plants will grow in your garden best.

PLANTS THAT ARE FUN TO GROW   Some sorts of ferns

and vines are pretty sure to grow. Morning glories, geraniums, snake plant, cultivated or wild asters, cacti of various kinds, and bulbs such as tulip or hyacinth should thrive when planted carefully at the right time.

One can have fun with even a windowsill garden of one or two 1- or 2-pound coffee cans, by trying to grow many things from seed to repotted plants and flowers. For instance, lentils, started in a very little water in a saucer, will soon become a miniature forest. Orange, grapefruit, lemon, or avocado seeds will usually grow into a small bush or tree. Try planting a piece of potato with an eye on it, a whole small sweet potato, which can become a big vine, a grain of fresh corn, or a carrot, beet, or horseradish top, with the greens cut back to within an inch from the top and about an inch of the root left on. These can be rooted in plastic bowls or glass jars containing only water, and planted later in pots with soil. Experiment with planting a little root of wild daisies, clover, buttercups, black-eyed Susans, or ivy. Some of these will continue to grow and flourish in your miniature garden.

Nature's Balance

People feel uneasy when they are off balance. Being off balance can be caused by many things such as food, surroundings, or a headache. They find it more difficult to do things easily and well until whatever caused their lack of balance has been corrected. Nature too can suffer greatly when unbalanced and, like people, does not feel well until the situation has been put right again.

It is very wrong to upset nature's balance. Who upsets it? Most of us do! How? There are many answers. A few are given below. There may be many more, depending on where and how you live and how much you get out into the woods and open spaces.

UPSETTING NATURE'S PLANS   Anyone can upset the balance of nature by:

- polluting water in any way, whether it be a pond, river, lake, or even the sea. In the case of the sea or a great river, it takes longer to pollute the water, so that it can be used neither by man nor fish.
- cutting down trees or destroying bushes or plants needlessly.
- gathering some rare species of wild flowers, which may prevent them from blooming again.
- moving rocks or big stones, without useful purpose, in a stream or river.
- stamping down an overhanging bank into a stream.
- running or walking up and down the same part of a grassy bank too often instead of zigzagging. Killing the grass and wearing a sort of deep path or trench in the earth can cause erosion.
- killing any of nature's creatures, whether animal, bird, or useful insect. Killing a dragonfly, for example, saves the lives of countless mosquitoes, flies, and other insect pests; killing toads, frogs, and many species of snakes has the same result.
- digging a ditch to drain water from a marsh or swamp, which makes it impossible for waterfowl to nest there.

Man is always interfering with nature's plans, and she is kept constantly busy setting things right, in her fight to maintain the right balance. Her work is very important to all of us because without it even insects could take up so much room on earth that there would be no place for us to live.

FOOD CHAINS   What does nature do to maintain her balance? The main answer is food chains. If there were no green plants, there could be no animals, nor could there be plants such as mushrooms and many other plants which are not green. Green plants can manufacture their own food, making sugar from water and carbon dioxide. The plants get their energy to do this from sunlight. They lock up some of the sunlight energy in the sugar, for use later on. Nearly all animals, whether small as gnats or big as elephants, get the necessary food by eating green plants.

These food chains, also called food webs, usually have from two to five links. One of the best known is the acorn-mouse-owl

ACORN-MOUSE-OWL FOOD CHAIN

chain. An even shorter one is the plankton-whale chain. Another chain begins with tiny plant lice which suck the sap of pine trees. These lice are eaten by spiders which, in turn, are eaten by small birds which are eaten by hawks. Since the pine wood area has no bird or animal which can eat a hawk, the hawk is known as the top carnivore, the last link in the food chain.

THE WORK THAT TREES DO   Trees play an important part in maintaining nature's balance. Not only are they green plants which manufacture their own food and supply food to animals but they protect the fertility of the soil by preventing erosion and thus make it possible for other green plants to grow.

To find out how much you really know about trees, try taking the following quiz (the answers are given at the end of the quiz).

TREE MAGIC QUIZ

1. When did the first tree grow?
2. Why are trees important to man?
3. How do trees keep diaries?
4. How do trees grow?
5. How much of a tree is alive?
6. How is the size of a tree measured?
7. How long are the roots of a big tree?
8. What is inside a tree seed?
9. What is a tree's top secret?
10. What happens when tree factories shut down?

ANSWERS TO TREE MAGIC QUIZ

1. Trees first balanced on their complex roots some 420,000,000 years ago.
2. Trees not only give man fresh air, food, and shade but they also influence the amount of rainfall and prevent floods. Wood from trees is used to make fires and to build houses, furniture, ships, and many other things. From wood pulp and fiber paper is made for printing, wrapping, and packaging. Trees have played an important part in world history and in developing America.
3. Though trees appear big, strong, and hardy, they are sensitive to weather conditions, injuries of any sort, and any attempt to push them around. They keep secret diaries which tell of their good times and hard times. Foresters can read these diaries by studying the rings inside a tree. In the happiest years of a tree's life, with ample rainfall, the rings are broad and evenly spaced, but in the years when a tree has suffered damage from drought, injury of some sort, or an attack by insects such as the sawfly, the rings are narrow and closer together.
4. Trees grow mainly from their crowns; a branch which is six feet above the ground today will still be six feet above ground in thirty years, though the tree will have grown much higher during that time.

5. Though only about 1 per cent of the total bulk of a tree is really alive, it fights hard to heal any damage done to it in order to remain healthy and flourish.

6. This is how to tell the size of a tree. Its bigness is defined by the area of three dimensions: height; circumference of the trunk, measured four and a half feet from the ground; and one quarter of the spread of the crown.

7. A big tree has hundreds of miles of roots to anchor it to the soil. These roots not only hold the tree in place but also bind the soil and prevent erosion which, without trees, ruins so much valuable land.

8. A tree seed contains a miniature tree complete with tiny leaves, stem, and tiny root tip, set in a food supply called endosperm. Once the root tip enters the soil, the pygmy tree is not only rooted but the tree is also able to absorb water and mineral food.

9. Every tree is a complicated factory, in action day and night, manufacturing sugar and that mysterious substance called chlorophyll. Scientists and manufacturers have spent millions of dollars in research, searching for chlorophyll without result, because they believe that this miracle green substance can be used in making medicines, dye, and food.

10. Even trees require rest, so in fall each broad-leaved tree which sheds its leaves each fall shuts down its astonishing factory for the winter. In late fall the cold weather seals off the leaves from the tree with a corklike substance so that the tree will be able to live through the cold winter weather. With the tree factory closed, the green color, chlorophyll, disappears and the yellow, orange, red, and purple colors, called carotene, which have been in the leaves all along, begin to appear. This change, especially in oaks and maples, brings a blaze of color to the landscape and is one of nature's most spectacular exhibitions.

HOW SEEDS SPREAD THEMSELVES   How does nature make sure that trees and other plants are widely distributed? People and animals help nature to sow her seeds, even if they

HOW FOUR PLANTS SOW THEIR SEEDS

Upper left: burdock seeds hitchhike. *Upper right:* violets shoot seeds. *Lower left:* tick trefoil seeds hitchhike. *Lower right:* dandelion seeds fly.

do not realize that they do so. Here are a few ways in which you have probably acted as a seed sower and carrier: blowing the fuzz of a dandelion, milkweed, or thistle, into the air; throwing any fruit pits on the ground while in camp or while holidaying in the country; touching witch hazel, wild violet, or jewelweed, either purposely or accidentally, in the fall when their seedpods were ready to expel their seeds with a pop!

One almost certain way in which many boys sow unpleasant, hitchhiking seeds, with the help of their dogs, is carrying seeds of the burr and hook family from these plants in one place to another. The names of these common burrs, armed with spines and hooks, are: burdock, cocklebur, tick trefoil, and beggar-ticks.

Seeds are designed to be sewn and create new plants. They use all kinds of ways to have man and beast, as well as water (if the seed can float) and wind (if the seed can be airborne), help them with the task of reproducing and multiplying.

Learning About the Earth

Geology deals not only with the structure of the earth's crust but also with the composition and development of its various layers. Other divisions of geology are mineralogy, the study of minerals, and petrology, the study of rocks, which includes rocks, stones, fossils, and the like. Many thousands of boys, and grownups too, who may know little of any of these sciences, are avid rock hounds and collect, polish, and sometimes cut many kinds of stones, from small pieces up to and including small rocks. Rocks and minerals are of great importance in our daily lives; we would not even have anything to walk on without them.

You might have to wait for months for various kinds of birds to return or for wild flowers to come up and blossom, but you do not have to wait to see rocks or minerals. On side roads, in parks, in banks of soil and stones, on corner lots, and in other places, one is likely to find stones and rocks of interest and beauty. Though outcrops of rocks are often seen in some states —New England and the Southwest, for instance—in the middle states thick soil makes it very difficult to find outcrops of rock unless they are looked for along river valleys and steep hillsides. People in various parts of the United States, and all over the world, are walking on different geological formations.

THE GEOLOGICAL HISTORY OF YOUR NEIGHBORHOOD The history of the place where you live is written in rocks, stones, and minerals of various sorts, but a little knowledge about geology and alert observation is needed to decipher that history. If there are ridges or cliffs, the steep bank of a river, or man-made exposures of rocks and minerals around where you live—and there is almost certain to be one of these sources of learning about the land—you can start right out as an amateur geologist. Quarries are fine sources of geological knowledge, but be sure to get permission to explore them and find out whether they are perfectly safe before looking around in them.

By borrowing or buying one of the fine paperback books which make the study of geology easy, an enterprising outdoors adventurer will be able to interpret the landscape and read the dramatic happenings of the amazing history of the earth, of which he is an inseparable part.

Today, more than ever before, minerals open up new and vital discoveries in technology and the sources of energy. Our forefathers and the American Indians hiked many hundreds of miles in their search for flints, spear points, and arrowheads. Today, in the space age, the hunt for valuable minerals and other products of the earth still goes on.

EQUIPMENT FOR ROCK HUNTERS The simplest gear required, where rocks and mineral lodes are broken, are a pair of heavy gloves, a knapsack or other stout bag, a notebook and pencil, and an old newspaper in which to wrap the specimens which you collect. Take also a few strips of adhesive paper or small labels, for writing the field identification, location, and

GEOLOGIST'S PICK

date. Some stones, rocks, and minerals are worth collecting simply for their beauty, others for the stories which they tell.

If you are near any hunting ground where specimens must be dug out of a bank or hillside, a geologist's pick or a plasterer's hammer and an old cold chisel are needed. A magnifying glass can be useful for collecting in the field, but it is even more handy at home. Choose well when you are collecting specimens and keep only a few of them, to start with. Specimens which weigh only a few pounds early in the day seem to weigh a ton after a long hike. In many cases, boys prolong the search for minerals and rocks into a lifelong quest, and quite often rock hounding proves a valuable hobby.

CHAPTER 3

Getting Acquainted With Nature's Creatures

USUALLY, ANIMALS AND birds are so shy and afraid of people that they keep out of sight and are rarely observed. The best way to meet these wild things is to help them to meet you.

Pointers for Observing Wildlife

To observe the squirrels, chipmunks, woodpeckers, blue jays, thrushes, robins, and starlings which may be in a park, sit quietly on a seat, log, or rock at the edge of a wooded clearing and let your eyes do some keen scanning. Any abrupt movement, even of a hand, though completely noiseless, will scare the wildlife.

When on the lookout for blackbirds, gulls, ducks, and other waterfowl, sit quietly in the shadows on the quietest wooded side of a pond, lake, reservoir, or stream.

WHEN TO SCOUT FOR WILDLIFE   Of course, boys who know when to look for various birds and animals will be more successful in their spying activities than those without this knowledge. Unfortunately, most animals and birds which one might see are active chiefly at dawn and dusk.

Nature, as well as human communities, is governed by a clock. Night and day are very good examples of the distinct division of nature's clock. During daylight, for instance, many birds, animals, and insects are busy and on parade. At dusk, when these daylight denizens are heading for home and sleep, the night roamers and fliers are getting ready for a working night, because all of these creatures work hard to enjoy life and find food.

Certain creatures are not only restricted to certain periods of the day or night but also to certain hours in these periods. If all of the night-flying insects took to the air at the same time, instead of working in distinct shifts, there would be no room for the millions of wings to navigate.

SNEAKING UP ON NATURE'S CREATURES Stalking animals and birds is a very difficult thing to do. Their sight, hearing, and built-in protective instincts are so very much greater than ours that we are at a great disadvantage when we try to match our stealth with theirs. It's possible to see much more by advancing as quietly as possible and taking advantage of the cover offered by tree trunks and bushes, but it's a sure thing that you are being observed far more than you are able to observe.

NATURE'S CAMOUFLAGE Thanks to nature's camouflage, animals and birds blend and "melt" into their natural surroundings. In this case, camouflage is really the natural, protective coloring of beasts, birds (females, as a rule), and insects. It gives near-perfect protection from their enemies.

Protective coloring shields wild creatures of all shapes and sizes, ranging from elephants to snakes and insects. Often body shapes and forms give additional protection to hide birds, beasts, and insects from their enemies.

FREEZING Often, hunted creatures see or sense their enemies, human or animal, pass nearby but, in such circumstances, the quarries rarely betray their presence by the slightest movement or sound. They "freeze."

Outdoors people, taking a cue from bird and beast, have learned to freeze too. Freezing is the art of remaining motionless and soundless at a moment's notice. Even if wild creatures have observed you, freezing will still encourage them to come cautiously out of hiding, and newcomers will pay little or no attention to you, so long as you remain frozen.

DECOYING WILDLIFE   This method of trying to observe wildlife sometimes proves a surer way of getting close to it than stalking. Certainly it is an easier way.

Hide in bushes or beside a brushpile, if there is one in the park, after scattering some suitable foods, such as unroasted peanuts, corn kernels, sunflower seeds, and even small pieces of bread, on the ground and on tree trunks and logs. Spread the food out fifteen feet or so from the edge of a clearing or in other spots which give the wildlife some cover, though still within your range of vision. Sooner or later this food will attract animals and birds, bringing them out of cover. Since wildlife is suspicious and hard to decoy, it takes much patience, at times, to get results.

Another way to try your hand at observing birds and beasts is to visit them instead of waiting until they visit you. Often, this method of attracting certain creatures gets results, provided there are animals living in the area. All animals have a streak of curiosity in their makeup. Here are some ways to arouse it:

- Tapping with a hardwood stick on the trunk of a den tree, generally recognized by its holes up and down the trunk. This may bring a squirrel, chipmunk, sleepy-eyed owl, or some other inhabitant of the tree to one of the windows or doors.
- Striking two pebbles lightly together can attract squirrels, chipmunks, and sometimes rabbits.
- A sucking noise, made with the lips on the back of a hand, often causes interest among smaller animals.
- A clicking sound, made with the mouth and lips, often draws attention.

- Squeaking with the lips will cause a few small animals to take notice.
- The gentle notes of a bird whistle will sometimes draw a response from an interested animal, perhaps a squirrel or chipmunk, as well as a bird. (Bird whistles are inexpensive and can be bought from the Audubon Society and in some stores.)

The calling should be carried out close to fallen trees or logs, brushpiles, and the trunks of live trees.

Attracting Birds

If you live in a city or suburb, and there are birds in that area, it may be possible to attract birds to your house. Bird food of some sort is the easiest way to bring some birds to a windowsill.

WINDOWSILL FEEDING STATIONS Try putting out bread crumbs, small pieces of suet, seeds of various sorts, such as sunflower, hemp, or millet, and a little shallow pan with fresh water in it. Of course, the birds that come to a windowsill feeding station will nearly always be sparrows, with perhaps a few starlings or even finches, depending on the locality. Pigeons are likely to come too, but they have dirty habits and are apt to become a nuisance.

NESTING BOXES The smaller birds which are found in and around urban areas will sometimes nest in almost any sort of little covered wooden box which is put out for them. A small wooden box, about half the length of a shoe box but the same width, with the lid fastened on and a small, round hole about 1½ inches in diameter cut in one end of it, may attract a sparrow or other small bird to a quiet window ledge or rooftop. A little dry grass, hay, or straw placed in the box will be used for nesting material. When one has a little yard which birds can get into easily and where a nesting box is not likely to be disturbed by cats or humans, an ideal place for such a box (which may attract

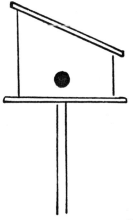

HOMEMADE NESTING BOX

finches or martins) is on top of a pole, 15 or 20 feet above ground. The box can be a small square or oblong wooden one, with a small hole cut in one end and some nesting material placed inside. It should be nailed securely onto the top of a pole or post set into the ground.

Sometimes it takes a long time for any species of bird to nest in a box in a city or town, though sometimes whole flocks of birds will decide to nest in a big colony in some city or town where nesting boxes have been set up by the citizens.

Neighborhood Birds

It may seem strange to find birds in urban areas, but birds such as sparrows, robins, starlings, and perhaps blackbirds and finches, are likely to be found almost anywhere. Such birds are apt to build nests in the roofs of houses, holes in buildings, city parks, small wooded areas, and the like. These may be the hiding places of many birds, and during the bird migration periods they are among the places most likely to be occupied by roosting birds and those resting and preparing to fly farther on. Some species of hawks and falcons (which are certainly among the wildest of birds) nest on New York City skyscrapers.

SPARROWS   A number of species of this little bird are to be found almost everywhere, even in and around densely populated areas. Among them the English sparrow, also known as the house sparrow, is too well known to need much description. The commoner species are usually buff, gray, and brown and range in length, including tail, from 5 1/2 to 6 1/2 inches. Their eggs, usually five or six, about 1/2 inch by 3/4 inch, are grayish-white, evenly speckled with brown. The eggs of other species of sparrows are often white, usually without markings. The nest varies according to where it is located. In built-up areas, it may be a hole in a wall, filled with grass, rags, paper, and feathers. In open country and parks, sparrows build in bushes, vines, and trees. The nest is a bulky dome of grass, straw, feathers, and rags, with a small entry hole on one side.

STARLINGS   These handsome, plump, short-tailed birds reflect a rainbow of colors from their glossy, dark plumage. They range from 7 1/2 to 8 1/2 inches in length and are aggressive, driving many other birds, even blackbirds, out of a territory which they take over. The female lays 4 or 5 pale blue eggs, about 1 1/4 inches long and 3/4 inch in diameter. Their nests are built in cavities in trees or buildings. The hole is filled with small sticks, straw, and grass, which are lined with softer grass and feathers.

BLACKBIRDS   The blackbird, which is about 9 inches long, is often found in cities or parks. Most blackbirds are of the species known as Brewer's. They are blackish, without the striking scarlet and gold shoulders of the red-winged blackbird, which is about 9 1/2 inches long and usually lives in freshwater and marsh areas. The yellow-headed blackbird, nearly 10 inches long, has a bright yellow head and neck, and is found in the marshes of the West where tall vegetation flourishes in deep water. The female Brewer's blackbird may lay 4 to 6 grayish eggs, 1 inch by 3/4 inch, usually heavily splotched with brown. Its nest is a hard cup of mud or clay, lined with grasses, hair, little roots, and feathers. Nests of Brewer's blackbirds are built at varying heights, from the ground to high up in trees. The other species build cup- or basket-like nests over the water, supported by thick reeds or suspended from marsh reeds.

ROBINS These big, plump, 10-inch-long birds are often seen in parks and on patches of grass in city and suburban areas. They sometimes prefer life in a residential area, rather than on the borders of a wood. Adult males are easily recognized by their reddish-brown breasts. The female lays from 3 to 5 blue-green eggs, without markings. They nest from 6 to 16 feet above ground, in dense bushes, thick trees, or sheltered recesses in buildings. The nest is usually built where it will not be rained on and is made chiefly from plant stems and odds and ends, cemented inside with mud into a smooth, solid cup.

Exploring the World of Insects

Because most insects are tiny, it is difficult for some people to be greatly interested in the wonderful lives of these creatures, though more than 640,000 different sorts of them share this world with us. Some boys regard insects as "just bugs," but scientists have learned so much that is useful to man by studying insect ways that they consider insects amazing creatures. Many people might be surprised to know that many insects, including butterflies and moths, tired after a hard day's work, sleep in the same place night after night and raise quite a fuss if some other insect tries to take over their home. A favorite sleeping shelter for butterflies and moths is under a log or in a fold in the rough bark of a tree.

LURING NIGHT-FLYING INSECTS Boys who wish to see insects at close range may lure them by lights, if they choose colors which the insects like. A light to medium shade of blue is the best color, but white will also attract most flying insects. A piece of light blue tissue paper or thin transparent blue cloth, tied over the end of a flashlight, will lure more insects than a white beam.

Some insects, sometimes found in parks, are also equipped with little flashlights which decoy humans. Fireflies, both male

FIREFLY

and female, have these built-in luminous fluid lamps which they flash on and off at will. These harmless, gunmetal-colored beetles have strong, protective wing covers, beautifully decorated with yellow borders. A little yellowish-white spot on the end of the body close to the tail is flash beam, from which its lovely greenish-yellow light glows.

Scientists are still trying to solve the problem of the firefly's "cold" light. When and if this is discovered, it will be a tremendous step forward in the field of lighting.

Quizzes

Most boys discover that there is no better way to find out how much or how little they know than by a self-quiz. Test this method out by trying to answer the questions in the following two quizzes.

POND LIFE QUIZ   This quiz deals with life in and above a pond. After you take the test, follow up by taking a close look at the nearest pond. The answers are given at the end of the quiz.

1. What is the very oldest plant seen growing on the surface of a pond?
2. Think of one wonderful pond insect which is even better equipped than a scuba diver and of its gear, which makes it a leader among all divers. Which is it? Why does it row in a zigzag pattern?
3. What hungry plants may be seen on the water in many ponds or growing on nearby marshy ground, waiting for a meal?
4. Which insect draws attention by its remarkable shadow patterns as it glides along the surface of the water with surprising speed?
5. The days when knights were bold have long passed. Yet, in many ponds, at certain times, busy little armorers are on the bottom making suits of armor for themselves. What is the name of this armorer and of what does he make his coat of mail?
6. Which insect, which may make watchers giddy with its antics on the surface of a pond, has two entirely different skills, besides having double eyes?
7. Name two common flying insects which are good friends of man. Why are they considered good friends?
8. What two insects have triggered inventions of use to man? One is big and savage, but friendly to man, and able to do something which no other insect among the half-million species can do. The other is rightly considered a pest.
9. What colors of lights do most insects dislike? They avoid two colors especially, and you can prove this by tying pieces of tissue paper of these colors (one at a time, of course) over the light-projecting end of a flashlight, on a dark night, and shining the light where insects are to be found.

ANSWERS TO POND LIFE QUIZ
1. Probably the oldest plants in the world are green algae, masses of living cells, on the surface of some ponds. Though you can see them, you cannot see most of the tiny creatures of the pond, feeding on the algae, just as cattle eat grass.
2. Water boatmen, equipped with wonderful air film or air bubble diving suits, row erratically, partly in order to cover

more water, to increase their chances of finding a meal, and partly to avoid becoming one themselves.

3. Bladderworts, which are insect-eating plants.

4. Water striders, supported by water tension, seem to skate along the surface of the water.

5. Caddis worms, busy on the bottom of ponds, make themselves suits of armor from particles of sand, pieces of pebbles, tiny twigs, and other minute material to protect themselves from enemies. This armor would be very uncomfortable if the caddis worm did not weave himself a silken undershirt, like a tube, to wear next to his body. He spins this silken case with his mouth, while holding the case in place with little hooks in his tail.

6. The whirligig beetle can dive, swim, and fly. He uses the upper part of his eyes above water and the lower part below water.

7. Insects such as the praying mantis, dragonfly, bee, ladybird beetle, caterpillar hunter, and some small wasps are friends to man. The praying mantis and dragonfly catch and eat many insects, such as mosquitoes and flies, which bite or annoy man. Besides making honey, bees pollinate fruit blossoms, so that trees bear fruit. Ladybird beetles eat aphids which destroy many flowering and fruit-bearing plants and fruit-tree crops. Caterpillar hunters and some small wasps devour insects or spiders which are annoying or harmful to man.

8. The praying mantis, which makes a good pet, is the friendly insect. It can look over its shoulder. Scientists learned a lot about inventing thermos bottles by studying the woven, foamy egg sacs of the praying mantis. The nuisance is the mosquito. Scientists discovered a great deal, when working on inventing unsinkable boats, by studying egg rafts of mosquitoes.

9. Red and yellow lights are unpopular in the insect world.

FACT AND FANCY QUIZ   There are many fancies regarding nature, but fact proves that most of them are fantasies.

Which of the following widely held notions are true? (Answers are given at the end of the quiz.)

1. The age of a rattlesnake can be told by the number of joints in its rattle.
2. Some snakes, such as the mud snake, take their tails in their mouths and roll downhill like a hoop.
3. The female cuckoo is the only bird which lays its eggs in the nests of other birds.
4. Gulls are so smart that they can recognize their nests among hundreds of other nests which look exactly alike.
5. That skillful engineer, the beaver, knows where each tree he fells will fall.
6. Squirrels always remember where they bury the nuts they gather.

ANSWERS TO FACT AND FANCY QUIZ

1. False. A rattlesnake adds a new joint to its rattle every time it sheds its skin, which may be three or four times a year.
2. False. A western lizard does take the end of its tail in its mouth, forming a hoop with its body, only when attacked by a snake. The snake, finding no end to the lizard, is robbed of a meal.
3. False. The female cowbird does exactly the same thing. Fortunately, the "bird-brained" wrens, catbirds, and robins spot the big cowbird eggs, puncture them, and heave them out of their nests. The yellow warbler even builds another nest bottom on top of the original one and lays her eggs or places her young in the new home.
4. False. They cannot tell their own eggs apart from those of other birds and will enthusiastically try to hatch a duck or goose egg which has been substituted for the original.
5. False. Beavers do not know which way the trees will fall. In fact, many beavers have been crushed under the trees which they felled.
6. False. Had squirrels known where their buried walnuts were hidden, the first settlers in America would not have found nut trees awaiting their arrival.

CHAPTER 4

All
Aboard!

TODAY, MANY BOYS use some sort of boat on some sort of water, and these amateur seamen get as much fun out of rowing or sailing odd, makeshift craft as experienced sailors do at the wheel of fine power boats. Many captains who sail proud ships on the seven seas started their sailing careers in rowboats and sailing dinghies on ponds and lakes. Boys who want to be sailors should practice the arts of watercraft aboard anything that floats and navigates safely whenever they get the chance. One good way to get practice in boating (though it may mean that an older boy or grownup will have to go along) is to rent a rowboat from a boathouse at a pond in a park.

Developing Water Skills

Any water skill should be developed slowly and carefully. It is too risky to use the trial-and-error method in learning boating, especially sailing and canoeing. One need not try to become a fine swimmer, to start with, but a boater must learn, through gaining confidence, not to fear the water or even mind being unexpectedly tipped overboard. For this, he should learn to float on his back and be able to swim at least twenty yards, either by the dog-paddle method or, much better, the breast stroke.

A poor swimmer has about the same chance in a boat upset as an expert swimmer, provided he keeps his head and stays with the boat or whatever craft he is using. The expert swimmer may misjudge the distance to shore, set out to swim to it, tire, and drown on the way. He runs a much greater risk than the poor swimmer who hangs onto the boat until rescued. Whatever happens, a beginner boatman should not panic.

A novice should never go out in a boat alone. For the first few weeks, while learning to navigate, he should go along with someone (an adult or an older boy) who has experience in rowing, sailing, canoeing, or whatever branch of watercraft he is trying to learn. He should also wear a life jacket when practicing.

Right from the start, a beginner should learn each navigating skill as well as he possibly can. If he learns to row sloppily, use a paddle incorrectly, or handle the tiller of a sailing dinghy or rowboat clumsily, it will take him longer to correct these bad habits later on than it will to develop these skills correctly in the first place.

Waterfaring Togs

Old clothes, and as few of them as possible, are best for one who is learning any branch of waterfaring. He not only has a good chance of getting wet, but also there may be tar or varnish which gets onto clothing (especially good clothing) very easily. An old shirt, with short sleeves, and a pair of shorts are fine wear for a seaman afloat or ashore, if he is already sun-tanned. Otherwise he had better wear long sleeves and slacks. Non-skid sneakers make good footwear. A sailor may prefer to go barefoot, when he is not a tenderfoot, but carry shoes along to wear ashore. Of course, one usually needs a warm wool sweater and/ or a windbreaker for cold weather. A good seaman is careful to keep himself warm.

Types of Small Craft

Whether he decides to navigate a raft, rowboat, kayak, or canoe, a boy has a lot of fun in store. Following are some pointers on what to look for in such craft.

RAFTS   Today, provided there are a few sound, buoyant logs floating or ashore at the edge of a pond or lake, a boy can build a serviceable raft which will carry one or more passengers. The only expense is the cost of a few big nails and some strong twine. String or twine serves better and lasts longer when it is dipped in oil of some sort or coated with paraffin wax.

The first thing to know about almost any raft of any size is that it is not buoyant enough to carry half as much weight as the builder hopes it will! It requires four logs about eight feet long and seven or eight inches in diameter to carry one boy. Usually, a fair-sized raft such as this will carry two passengers if they sit on the logs with their feet dangling in the water. Of course, empty tin cans, with the lids fastened on with waterproof adhesive tape, can be tied on the foot of the raft, at each corner, to give added buoyancy, but such cans are not easy to find just when you want them, so let's stick to logs.

Good logs should be about eight feet long and from six to ten inches in diameter. Two, four, or more of these logs are floated side by side in the water at the shore edge. Then they are lashed together with rope, cord, or strong twine or string, or nailed together by means of crosspieces of various lengths and thicknesses. Crosspieces do not need to be thick, provided they are tough and strong. They can be laid crossways on the logs or in the form of an "X" that crosses all of the logs.

If two or three boys want to ride on a raft which is not buoyant enough to carry them, a space of ten inches or so may be left between the logs so that the rafters' feet and legs dangle in the water. A bathing suit or an old pair of shorts is suitable for rafting.

Another sort of raft may be built with ponchos, squares of waterproof canvas, tarps, or pup-tent halves. These are tightly rolled and tied around bundles of twigs or even dry grass. Such

BULLBOAT-TYPE RAFTS

Left: brush framework. *Right:* completed raft.

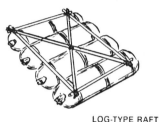

LOG-TYPE RAFT

This raft is made from ponchos, canvas, tarps, etc., tightly rolled and tied around bundles of twigs or dry grass, in the shape of logs. An individual "log" is shown at left.

rafts can be made in the form of a lifebuoy or an Indian bullboat, as illustrated. They may also be made in the form of logs, as shown in the drawing. These rafts, when well made so that they are really waterproof, float easily and are lightweight when they have to be transported.

The bullboat type of raft is made from stout 3½-foot-long poles, held in place by withes woven around and in between them. The ends of these poles, which are driven into the ground for about a foot, should be sawed off after the sides have been woven. To complete the raft, a strong stick floor is tied into the bottom. Of course, this raft will not be waterproof or very buoyant, since it is supposed to support only the weight of the raftsman who is on board. Without the floor, the raft is used with the passengers' feet and legs dangling in the water.

Rafts tip and tilt and are the sort of craft that one uses for fun or for emergency purposes. They are easier to push with a pole than paddle, though both paddle and pole can be used to advantage aboard a good raft.

ROWBOATS   Here are fine craft for beginning boatmen.

ALL ABOARD! • 49

They come in nearly all shapes and sizes. They can be rowed, paddled, poled, and sailed, with a maximum of safety, provided they are seaworthy. A seaworthy craft is one which is built well, balances well, and is watertight. A boat which has all these qualities and is lightweight is still better. There are so many used boats for sale these days that a fairly good craft can be had quite cheaply, especially if two fellows club together and buy half-shares in a boat. Such a seafaring partnership not only reduces the cost, but there are four hands instead of only two to patch, paint, and equip the boat.

Also in the rowboat class, the round-bottomed dinghy is seaworthy and fairly fast under oars, when a narrow-stern craft is chosen. This boat is also easy to handle under sail.

KAYAKS   This Eskimo type of craft is made of plastic and fabrics, these days, and there is also a fine folding model, made of rubberized canvas, which comes in one- and two-seater models. They fold into small space and can be assembled easily within one hour. The two-seater costs about half as much as a canoe and it has quite a few advantages. It is a stable craft and draws little water, so that it may be paddled by two boys in even less than two feet of water, when it is not too heavily loaded. Two boys can carry it for short distances without strain. There is quite a lot of room in the stern, under the canvas decking, to carry some camping and other gear. It is very useful for exploring narrow, shallow waterways where not even rowboats can navigate. With leeboards, it sails well.

CANOES   The canoe is a craft for older boys who are able to use great care in handling craft of any sort and have saved up enough money to buy a secondhand canoe. A good, stable canoe can cost quite a lot of money, but, when handled well, is a very safe craft. Though it requires more skill to paddle well than to row, a canoe is most maneuverable, light, and serviceable.

A canoe with a low bow and stern, a guide-type canoe, is safer than one with a high bow and stern, especially when it is windy. Modern canoes are often cedar frame jobs, covered with canvas, though some are made of fiber glass and reinforced plastic. There is also an aluminum model, which floats splendidly and requires little upkeep. It does ship more wind than a good wood-and-canvas model and is rather noisy, but it is still a good canoe for both ordinary canoeing and cruising. Quite a number of second-hand aluminum canoes are on sale these days, and they are easier to repair and maintain than most other sorts.

Soft-soled shoes, such as sneakers, should be worn when canoeing. One should never embark or disembark from a canoe until it is completely afloat.

Repairing Small Craft

Practically all boats, especially wooden ones, leak at some time or other, especially after winter storage. The trial-and-error method is the surest way to find seam and other leaks requiring repair. Here is how it works. In spring, one may submerge a wooden boat in water overnight, or even for a few days. This immersion causes the seams to swell so that the boat usually becomes watertight, unless there are some other sources of leaks which can be spotted and patched. Empty the craft and climb aboard it with one or two other boys to find out if it is still letting in water. If it is, and the places where the leaks occur can be found, sandpaper the boards around the leaks. When the boards are dry, caulk them with a mixture of rope fiber and tar or some good commercial caulking solution. Then patch them with round patches of waterproof cloth, such as canvas held in place with marine glue. Glue a few extra patches onto suspect spots—just in case.

EMERGENCY REPAIR KIT   Here is an emergency repair kit which can prove handy for minor emergency repairs to small craft. The items mentioned should be packed in a small, waterproof bag.

TOOLS

a pair of long-nosed pliers	a pair of scissors
a small hammer	an awl
a small screwdriver	a putty knife

about a yard of closely woven nylon or cotton cloth, for patches	some brass screws and small brass brads in assorted sizes
a roll of waterproof adhesive tape	a few pieces of sandpaper or emery cloth
a few feet of soft cotton or hemp rope (oakum) for caulking	a small can of marine glue
some thin copper or brass wire	about 20 feet of fish line
some varnish and a brush	

This kit can take care of the average temporary repairs required in making a rowboat, canoe, or other small craft watertight and also for carrying out other minor repairs.

Boating Safety

Safety is the most important part of boating in any craft, from rowboat to ocean liner. The saddest thing about boating accidents is that the great majority of them can be avoided. Most boating accidents are caused through carelessness. Sometimes someone thinks that what he should be doing is being done by someone else, or he thinks that the other boat will give him the right of way, which is exactly what the fellow in the other boat thinks too.

If carried out, the following rules may protect you from having a boating accident.

- *Never* take out any craft that is not seaworthy.
- *Never* go boating in any storm, especially an electrical one.
- *Never* overload or overpower a small boat or canoe.
- *Never* leave a small boat or canoe in case of an upset. *Stay with the craft.*
- *Never* clown around in any small boat or canoe.
- *Never* lean out of a canoe or small boat needlessly.
- *Never* stand up in a small boat or canoe.

- *Never* paddle or row after dark unless you absolutely must.
- *Never* change places needlessly in a small boat or canoe.
- *Never* sit on the foredeck or gunwales of a small boat or on the gunwales or thwarts of a canoe.
- *Never* accept responsibility for a non-swimmer aboard your small craft.
- *Never* carry out repairs to the hull of any small craft when bare-legged in cold water. The feet and legs can become so numbed that even bad cuts and bruises are not felt—until later!
- *Never* embark or voyage in a canoe or any other small craft that is not well trimmed. Trimmed is the nautical term for a boat which has perfect balance, both from a viewpoint of passengers and freight.

Cruising

When one lives in or close to most big cities, it is not easy to find ponds, lakes, or streams on which one can cruise for any distance. However, a fellow can get some very useful practice for later on, when chances for cruising do occur, by mini-cruising on whatever water is closest to his boat. This is necessary in order to keep expenses low, since it costs money to transport even a rowboat to a distant cruise starting point. Since some boys have rowboats or other craft and live close to a lake or river, it is helpful to know about possibilities close to home.

PLANNING THE CRUISE   First of all, even before working on a cruising plan, a prospective *voyageur* must make certain that his craft is in good shape. There should be no leaks, no sprung seams, no weakness in the boat structure, and the floor and/or floorboards should be strong and not in need of repair. Any fellow who gets around in a boat knows that the best place to make his craft seaworthy is at home, where he can find the tools necessary for making repairs.

One should plan the cruise in advance. Such an undertaking should not be started on the spur of the moment, and planning is fun too. The first question is how far you can go easily either by sail, oars, paddles, or small outboard engine. Remember also that if the whole cruising area covers only a few miles, it is wise to cover the entire distance in one day, during daylight, unless there is a good place where you are allowed to camp at the end of the first day. When there is, you can combine cruising with a little camping, instead of just overnighting, or bivouacking. Once the length of the cruise and the time to be spent on this adventure has been decided on, the paper work has been done, except for making a list of what you will need to eat and drink during the trip and also what sleeping gear and shelter for the night is required. The rations are few for a brief trip, and these are mentioned later in this chapter, along with sleeping gear.

After the supplies and gear have been stowed aboard, most of the food and other gear can be packed into the stern of most boats, with a little forward, in the bow, to help keep an even distribution of weight. Then the crew goes on board and casts off. Any cruise, even a half-day trip, is much safer and more fun if at least two fellows go together. A third or fourth may go along, provided the craft can easily carry that number of boys and there are ample rations to go around.

Even cruises on a large pond provide excellent practice in rowing, going ashore and shoving off again, and spending the night under the stars. Every member of the cruise should take turns in rowing and navigating, which includes picking the best places to go ashore when exploring or setting up a bivouac for the night. A cruise of this sort is a fine chance to share one's knowledge about watercraft with other fellows. They may learn a good deal about rowing, using a compass, and navigating from you, and you may learn as much or more from your fellow *voyageurs.*

Overnighting

It is fun and good practice for more advanced camping later on to spend a night or longer outdoors, sleeping under the stars. Not much sleeping gear is needed, especially if you own a sleeping bag. Basic equipment includes a poncho or ground sheet, a warm blanket or two less warm ones, a small cushion or pillow (or an empty pillowcase which can be filled with dry grass or the like and used as a pillow), a piece of strong plastic or weatherproof fabric about 6 x 12 or 8 x 16 feet (depending on how large a shelter you wish), and a few lengths of twine or cord. This completes the overnighting equipment, except for the few personal things, which include a pack, a flashlight, a good pocketknife, a canteen or thermos bottle, and a waterproof box of matches. A mess kit of some sort (or just a lightweight fork and spoon, a couple of paper plates, and a plastic cup) will take care of the usual overnighting dining needs.

FOOD THAT'S QUICK AND EASY   Not much variety is needed for one or two overnight meals, but there should be plenty to eat, since one gets hungry when voyaging. Some milk with a little ice added can be carried in a canteen or thermos for a while but does not keep well. It is better to take a hot drink such as cocoa or chocolate in a thermos bottle. Lemonade or fruit drinks are fine, but carbonated drinks will make the thermos explode. A few hearty sandwiches and apples or bananas for dessert make satisfactory meals.

It is not easy these days to find a place in suburbia where lighting fires in the open is allowed, but if you take along a portable cookstove, some easy-to-cook foods may be added to the rations. Portable stoves are available which burn solid fuel and fit into a big pocket or can be slipped into a pack.

Among easy-to-prepare foods are powdered soups, or, if there is stowage space on board, condensed canned soups. Milk for cooking can be taken either in powdered form or as evaporated milk when there is room for it. Hamburgers, frankfurters, canned chili con carne, Welsh rarebit (cheese cooked with milk), potato chips, and some raw vegetables such as carrots and celery may be taken along for variety. Dried figs, raisins, and prunes are fine desserts when overnighting.

SHELTERS   The plastic sheet or weatherproof cloth mentioned above, perhaps made of lightweight canvas or duck, is used to make a shelter for protection from rain or dew. Sewing or tying a strong cord or piece of tape about eighteen inches or two feet long to each corner, will make the shelter much easier to set up quickly. It is fastened to a convenient tree branch or slung over a rope fastened to a tree and pegged to the ground, as illustrated.

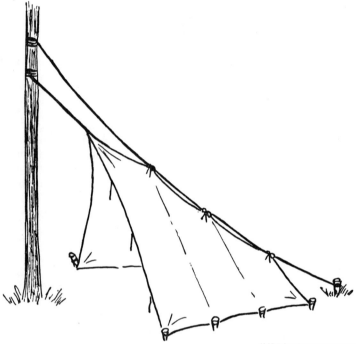

IMPROVISED SHELTER

CANOE AND TARP SHELTER

A shelter can also be made from a tarpaulin or plastic sheet and a canoe or rowboat, turned on its side and securely braced with long stakes so that it cannot fall over in the night. The canvas cover is fastened to the top side of the boat by cords coming over the boat from the opposite side or by cords held on the far side of the keel by a long, straight branch. The cover can also be fastened, in some boats, to the gunwale or oarlocks. One soon devises the best way for his craft. The lower side of the shelter is staked to the ground, forming, with the help of the boat, a lean-to shelter under which one can sleep dry.

CHAPTER 5

Getting
Ready For
Fishing Fun

FISHING IS AN exciting, challenging sport for all ages. It is an art which requires sportsmanship, patience, and a certain know-how, which can develop into a fine skill. A good angler must know not only fishing strategy but also the fish's strategy, since one often has to outwit its ruses in order to land it.

Fishing can be practiced and enjoyed in little pools and streams in parks or in rivers, lakes, bays, and oceans, depending on where you live and holiday. Fishing can become the favorite hobby of a lifetime, so it is well to begin as soon as possible. How about today?

What Fishermen Should Take Along

Practically any old clothes will do to fish in. They should be comfortable and loose-fitting. A sport shirt, preferably with long sleeves, and a pair of jeans are fine. Shorts and a T-shirt are comfortable when one is sun-tanned. In cooler weather, one should wear warm clothing, and a warm wool sweater, a mackinaw, or a windbreaker should be taken along. Sneakers or soft-soled moccasins are comfortable when fishing from a boat. If rough ground has to be covered, or the fishing spot is some distance from the starting point, good hiking shoes should be worn. But for complete comfort, sneakers or moccasins can be carried along to be worn when the fishing hole is reached. Heavy wool socks will keep the feet warm in cold weather.

Rubber boots of any length, used as waders, become very dangerous when they become filled with water and may drag even the best swimmer down.

A rather wide-brimmed old felt hat is handy on fishing trips. The brim helps to keep the sun out of the eyes, and the band around the hat is just the place to hang lures and flies. An old wide-brimmed straw hat can take its place. Most fishermen fish successfully in their bare heads.

PERSONAL GEAR   Handy things to take along on fishing trips are a pair of good sunglasses, an accurate compass, a good pocketknife, a length or two of strong and lightweight string, mosquito repellent, sunburn lotion, a small first aid kit, a sandwich or two, and a canteen filled with pure drinking water, or a thermos bottle filled with a favorite beverage.

BASIC FISHING NEEDS   Fishing gear includes everything from fishing poles and rods to artificial lures. The beginning fisherman needs all of the following items:

- a lightweight fishing line about thirty feet long.
- a small package of small hooks of various sizes, either snelled hooks (ones with a short length of gut or nylon attached) or ordinary hooks which have a little ring at the end to which the line is fastened.
- a lead sinker weighing about three ounces.
- a fishing pole from 6 to 10 feet long, such as an inexpensive bamboo one.
- some natural bait, preferably worms.

One other thing which will help to make your first fishing

expedition more exciting and interesting is a bobber, also known as a float or floater. It is used to support the weight of the line, hook, bait, and sinker at various depths.

All of this gear should not cost more than about one and a half dollars and it can be bought for less. A boy who lives in the country can, of course, cut his own fishing pole from a tree with springy branches, such as willow, but conservation laws make it difficult to cut a branch without getting into trouble, these days. A little money can also be saved by the boy who makes his own sinker and bobber, as described later in this chapter.

Handy Fishermen's Knots

A fisherman should not only know some worthwhile outdoor knots but also some of the most useful fishermen's knots. The basic outdoor knots are not hard to tie. They will not become undone under strain, but knotting with monfilament, nylon monofilament, and even nylon lines is much more difficult than merely knotting with string, cord, or rope. Here are some of the practical, all-purpose knots which fishermen should be able to tie surely, fairly quickly, and in difficult circumstances, such as in a rowboat when the water is choppy.

SQUARE KNOT (REEF KNOT)   The square knot is useful for joining two pieces of fishing line together. It's easy to tie. Look at the drawing a moment. Bring end A over end B, toward

SQUARE KNOT

you, under, and away from you. Then bring end B over end A, away from you, under, and toward you. Pull taut.

SHEET BEND   The sheet bend is even better way to tie

two pieces of line together, since there is less chance of its slipping when two lines of different thickness are joined. The drawing shows how easy it is to transform a square knot into a sheet bend.

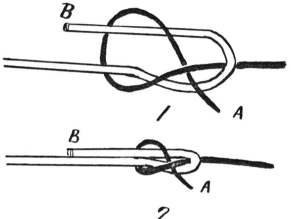

STEPS IN TYING THE SHEET BEND

To tie a sheet bend, first tie a square knot. Then pass end A *under* its standing part (the long part of the rope) and *over* the bight (curve) of the other rope, as in step 1. Pull taut, as in step 2.

CLOVE HITCH   This is a fine knot which can be made to

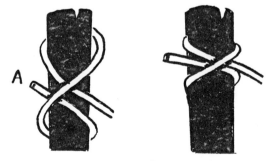

TYING THE CLOVE HITCH AROUND A POST
Left: hitch ready for tightening. *Right:* hitch pulled taut.

GETTING READY FOR FISHING FUN • 61

go around a pole or post of practically any size and will not slip. It is a good knot to tie a line onto a cane fishing pole and may also be used to join poles together or hitch a boat onto a mooring post or dock.

To tie this hitch place the rope around the pole or post with end A on the right. Then bring end A over the standing part, around the pole again, and under its bight, as shown. Pull taut.

To drop the rope over a low mooring post, hold the end of the rope being worked on in the left hand and form a loop as shown in A, then another beside it, as in B. Place the second

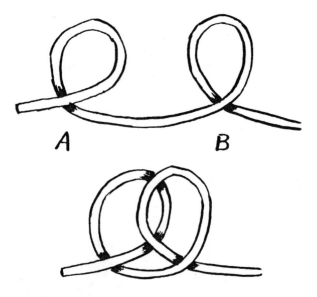

DROPPING THE CLOVE HITCH OVER A POST

loop over the first, as shown in C, and drop them over the post. Pull taut.

FISHERMAN'S KNOT   The fisherman's knot and the knots which follow are all good for tying monofilament, though the fisherman's knot is better for regular line knotting. To tie the fisherman's knot, make an overhand knot at the end of line A by passing the end *under* the standing part, around and *over* the standing part, then through the bight just formed. Now,

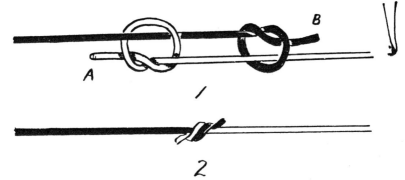

STEPS IN TYING THE FISHERMAN'S KNOT

pass the end of line B through the loop on line A and make an overhand knot in the end of line B so it comes around the standing part of line A, as shown in step 1. Pull the knot taut as in step 2.

CLINCH KNOT   The clinch knot is handy for tying a line to a fish hook. Thread the line through the eye of the hook.

CLINCH KNOT

Make a bight and three or four twists toward you; then slip the end through the bight at the hook. Pull taut.

IMPROVED CLINCH KNOT   This knot is made exactly as the one above except that five or more twists are made be-

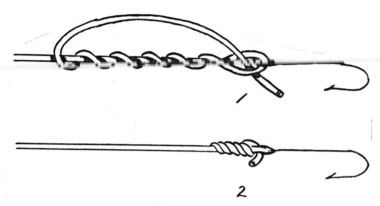

fore slipping the end through the bight, as in step 1, and pulling the knot taut, as in step 2.

BLOOD KNOT   Twist line A around line B three times, then thread the end *up* through, as in step 1. Now, twist line B around

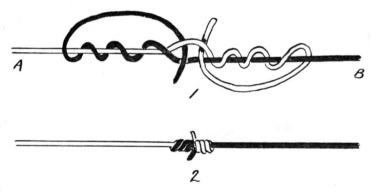

line A three times and tuck the end *down* through, as shown. Pull taut as in step 2.

END LOOP   Make a bight, as in step 1. Then bring it across

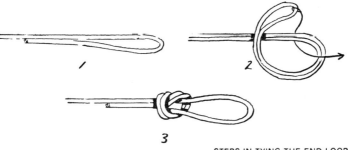

its standing part, as in step 2, and pull it around it and up through the bight just formed. Pull taut as in step 3.

JAM KNOT   Make an end loop (see its illustration) in end A. Then weave end B through the loop just formed, around behind

JAM KNOT

it, and down through it again. Make an overhand knot, as described under Fisherman's Knot, in the tip end of B. Pull taut.

FIGURE EIGHT   Make an end loop (see its illustration) in line A. Then weave line B up through the loop, around behind

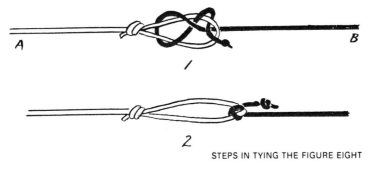

STEPS IN TYING THE FIGURE EIGHT

it and *under* its own standing part, over the side of the loop in A, then around it and *up* over its own standing part and over the bight in A, as in step 1. Pull taut as in step 2. An overhand knot at the up end, as described under Fisherman's Knot, makes this more secure.

INTERLOCKING LOOPS   Make an end loop (see its illustration) in end A. Then weave end B *down* through the loop, up around it, then across and under the other side of the loop.

A

B

Now bring the end B *up* through the loop, over the bight, and tie the end to its own standing part with an overhand knot (see Fisherman's Knot for how to tie an overhand knot).

Fishing Tackle

A boy who knows the handy fisherman's knots described above will have no trouble getting his fishing tackle in working order. He will easily be able to tie a line to a pole, leader, hook, sinker, or bobber. The information below will not only help a fellow decide what kind of tackle to buy but also tell how he can improve it and, in some cases, make his own.

FISHING LINES   One hundred yards of fishing line can cost from about a dollar to around twenty dollars and more, though there is about the same chance of catching fish with a cheap line as with an expensive one. Inexpensive lines, fine for still-fishing (discussed in Chapter 6), often come in 25- to 50-yard spools, and for catching panfish a 6- to 8-pound test line is heavy enough.

Fishing lines come rolled on spools, and the lengths vary from 25 to well over 100 yards, depending on the test weight and the sort of line. These range from heavy, braided lines to the near-invisible monofilament lines. When one intends to try for panfish and bigger fish, during a day's fishing, it is well to take along two spools of fishing line, one loaded with 4- or 6-pound test line and the other with 8- or 10-pound test line. The light line may be used for smaller fish and smaller lures, while the heavier line is used for heavier fish and larger lures.

REELS These useful gadgets can be very expensive, when equipped with all modern attachments, so many experienced fishermen get along very well with uncomplicated reels. They use skill instead of gadgetry and, for them, it works. However, a lightweight, free-spool reel, used with a 6- or 8-pound test line, equipped with a level-wind mechanism, which feeds the line evenly onto the spool, and an anti-backlash device, will usually prevent snarled and tangled lines. Reels are attached to the butt of a rod by two movable bands or, on expensive rods, by more complex devices.

LEADERS Leaders are 12-inch, and longer, lengths of strong, fine monofilament which have a barbed hook at one end and a small loop, for attaching the fishing line, at the other.

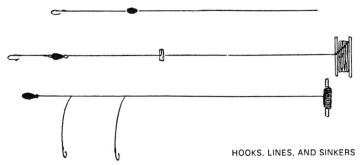

HOOKS, LINES, AND SINKERS

Leaders are stronger than any light line and are far less likely to be bitten through or break. Leaders have a double purpose: to make the attachment to the line as nearly invisible as possible and to make it difficult for some fish to cut or break it.

Today, many experienced fishermen do not use leaders because the monofilament line which they use is as fine and as invisible as good monofilament leaders.

SWIVELS AND SNAPS   Swivels come in many different sizes. They are used to keep the fishing line from becoming twisted and to foil fish movements. They are often attached

SWIVEL *(left)* AND SNAP *(right)*

between the leader and the line. Often, the swivels are attached to snaps, which are helpful in snapping on lures and baits speedily.

HOOKS   There are thousands of sorts of metal fish hooks, but only the best ones are effective. A Scandinavian hook maker manufactures 60,000 different types. One leading American hook manufacturer sells over 1,000,000 fish hooks a day. These hooks are made in countless shapes, sizes, lengths, strengths, points, and finishes. Such figures hint at the number of fish hooks which are lost, snagged, broken off, and carried off by fish daily.

Though many hooks look alike, some, including most hooks made in Norway, have sharper, better barbs, assuring more certain catches. Use the best hooks you can afford and ask your local dealer about the most effective sizes. He should know the sort of fish you are most likely to catch in your area and the best size of hooks with which to catch them. He can sell you packages of hooks of assorted sizes, snelled or with long or short unsnelled shanks, suitable for either cane-pole outfits or fine, modern fishing rods.

Snelled hooks are ones with a leader, a nearly invisible length of fine nylon or, better still, nylon filament, attached to the hook. Ordinary hooks are designed for the line to be attached directly to a tiny eye on the shank, the opposite end from the barb. However, a nylon or monofilament leader can also be

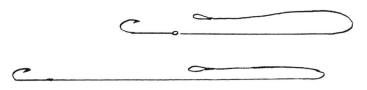

Top: hook and leader. *Bottom:* snelled hook.

tied securely to these eyes. These ordinary hooks can be had with long or short shanks, the longer shank being convenient to thread a worm onto. You can buy, or your dealer can give you, a little chart showing the correct hook sizes for catching various species of fish.

The smaller the hook, the better. Panfish and other small fish will rarely get caught on a large hook, but some quite big fish are often caught on smaller hooks. Suitable hook sizes for panfish are #12 to #4. For bigger bass and other larger fish, one can use sizes #4 to #1½, and so on up in size, depending on the size of the fish in a particular area.

DISGORGERS AND PLIERS   A disgorger is a very useful gadget. It is a short length of metal with a little fork on one end. When a fish has swallowed the hook deeply, the forked end of the disgorger is pushed down onto the hook so that the barb is driven through the part in which it is hooked and the hook can be extracted easily. Some fishermen use a pair of long-nosed pliers to loosen the hook. A disgorger can be made by flattening one end of a 6-inch length of metal coat hanger and then making a shallow notch in it with a file. Such a hanger can be twisted into a sort of ring or loop at the opposite end from the notch.

SPREADERS   A spreader, as illustrated, is a short, stiff wire arc, ranging from six to about twelve inches long, which offers a fisherman who is still-fishing (see Chapter 6) two chances of getting a bite, instead of one. The spreader shown is the sort which can be bought in a fishing tackle store, but one can easily be improvised in this way:

Bend a short length of lightweight coat hanger into the shape

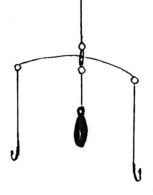

SPREADER

illustrated. Attach a small swivel to the end of the fishing line and, with a short piece of strong, thin twine or wire, securely fasten the spreader at the exact center to the lower ring of the swivel. The sinker is also attached to this ring. Attach a hook, on a short length of fish line, or better still, a length of monofilament leader, to the spreader at each end, to complete the gadget. It can also be made without using a swivel.

SINKERS   These are weights made to attach to the fishing line. They are made of lead or other metals, shaped so that they will not get caught easily on weeds, rocks, or other submerged objects. Improvised sinkers can be made of small stones, shaped so that the line will not slip off, nuts, bolts, or even heavy nails. One should use the smallest sinker possible in order to do the desired job. A lightweight sinker weighs two ounces or less. Larger sinkers are needed to offset strong currents and strong winds. Sinkers should generally be attached to a line so that they are a foot or so away from the bait.

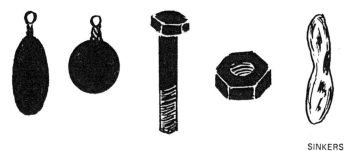

From left to right are two lead sinkers, a bolt, a nut, and a stone.

BOBBERS   The job of a bobber is to support the weight of the line, bait, and sinker, when the sinker is not on the bottom, and show when a fish is nibbling or grabbing. That is why a bobber adds fun and interest to fishing. When the fish makes off with the bait, the bobber moves fast in the same direction as the fish is traveling.

Bobbers should be as small as possible for the job they have to do. One can buy a bobber for a few cents, but improvised bobbers work very well and cost little or nothing. Among the homemade bobbers are corks of various sizes; old ping-pong balls, tied to the line with a clove hitch or attached to the line with a strip of waterproof adhesive tape; small plastic bottles

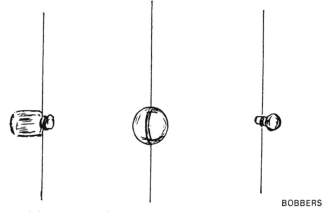

BOBBERS

Left: plastic bottle. *Center:* ping-pong ball. *Right:* flash bulb.

GETTING READY FOR FISHING FUN • 71

and tubes; short lengths of quill, with the ends plugged; used flashbulbs; and small, shaped pieces of lightweight wood, such as balsa and pine.

FISHING POLES AND RODS A bamboo fishing pole is also known as a cane pole. It is the easiest to get and is the least expensive, today. It may be bought in many hardware stores and in most stores which sell fishing supplies. The bamboo pole should be from 8 to 12 feet long, not too supple at the butt end, but supple enough at the tip end to show when you have a bite. The length of the pole should depend on where it is going to be used. For fishing from a boat or bridge, the pole need not be longer than 10 feet. However, if the fishing is to be done from the bank of a pond or stream with brush or weeds growing at the edge, the pole must be long enough to hold the line clear of these obstacles, to assure good fishing.

This fishing pole can be used by tying one end of a 40-foot length of 6- or 8-pound test braided cotton line securely to the butt end of the pole with a clove hitch covered by a square knot. The rest of the line is wound smoothly around the pole from butt to tip, to be used as spare line when needed, except for about 20 feet of line which may be left free at the tip of the rod, the line at that point being tied with a clove hitch around a small notch cut in the tip of the pole. A hook is tied about 8 to 10 inches above the end of the line, and a sinker, weighing 2 or 3 ounces, is tied onto the tip end of the line.

This is the very simplest method of fishing known today. There is little doubt that it is most effective; so many boys make fine catches of all sorts of fish with it. However, even beginners often add one more useful gadget to their lines—a bobber. The bobber is attached to the fishing line from 6 to 36 inches or so above the hook, allowing the baited hook to rest either right on the bottom of a pond or stream, or suspended several inches below the surface of the water being fished. The bobber shows when the bait is even being nibbled.

This rig can be improved without spending any money. A ring guide can be tied onto the very tip of the pole by using part of a stout paper clip or even the head of a strong hairpin. About

3/4 inch of wire is left on each side of the curve, when the paper clip or hairpin is being snipped to make a guide. Instead of resting content with this improvement, one can make three or four of these guides and bind them firmly onto the pole. The ends of each paper clip or hairpin should be turned up about

PAPER CLIP OR HAIRPIN GUIDES

Top: at tip of pole. *Center:* bent and ready to be tied to side of pole. *Bottom:* tied to side of pole.

3/8 inch, as illustrated, to serve as a ring through which the line passes, the shank of wire at each side being bound onto the pole and the guides spaced equal distances apart. The drawing shows how this can be done. Now, the beginner has a pole with guide rings and a guide ring on the tip, through which fishing line will run easily.

If you have, or can borrow, any old fishing reel which works, you can easily turn a cane fishing pole into a very good fishing rod by using two short pieces of strong cord and fastening the reel onto the butt of the pole with a clove hitch. Securely bind the reel about 4 inches from the end, by each metal projection, one on each side of the reel. (It is usually held in place on a fishing rod by a sliding band, one on each side of the reel.) Tie a clove hitch in the center of an 18-inch piece of strong string, binding the reel and pole securely together. Then wind the rest of the string tightly around the pole and reel and tie the two ends with a reef knot.

Provided one has the opportunity to use it fairly often, a real fishing rod is a fine thing to own. Such a rod may be equipped with end sections of various lengths and strengths for various kinds of fishing. These rods are made from cane of various sorts and qualities, including Tonkin cane; glass, hollow and solid, fiber glass; and various kinds of lightweight metals and alloys. A good rod should have a fairly flexible tip but enough "backbone" to battle a fighting fish. There is a terrific difference in the prices of rods, ranging from five or six dollars to several hundred dollars. This does not mean that expensive rods catch the most fish. If a boy chooses well, takes advantage of a good sale, and uses a good line and effective lures, he can catch as many fish with a rod costing only five to ten dollars as the fellow with three rods, two tackle boxes stuffed with lures and other gadgets, and two or three fishing reels, including one for spinning!

Baits

There are hundreds of baits, natural and artificial, but fortunately the average fisherman can get along and make good catches with only a few of them.

NATURAL BAITS Among the best all-around natural baits are worms and night crawlers. Other natural baits are live minnows, frogs, grasshoppers, grubs, beetles, locusts, mayflies, and others. Some insects which are useful to man, such as dragonflies, are much too valuable to use; while you fish, they are busy catching the mosquitoes which would otherwise feast on you!

Live bait is sometimes hard to find, these days, but a little ingenuity will often net a good supply of worms, night crawlers, and minnows.

Night crawlers are really king-size worms which come out from below their little mounds of earth at night to take a look around. They are so much in demand for bait that it is well to know how to attract them to the surface both night and day. Here is a hot tip that often works: Stir one tablespoonful of powdered mustard into a quart of water. Pour half a cupful of this liquid on top of the night crawler's mound. Often the crawler will be lured to the surface, and from there into the fisherman's bait can.

To lure worms to the surface, dissolve two tablespoons of detergent in a quart of warm water—hot water, if the ground is very cold. Then pour the water on the ground and watch. In a few minutes, if there are any worms in that area they will crawl out onto the surface. Rinse them off in clean, cold water as soon as possible after they are caught or the detergent will kill them.

An easy way to net minnows is with a soap decoy. Take a piece of soap which makes a good lather, and work up a lather in the water in a small area where minnows are to be found. Wait for a minute until the suds settle; then draw a minnow net through the lathered water and take the minnows which have been lured by the lather. Any suds will wash off the minnows when they are put into a can of fresh water.

Among other edible baits are small strips cut from the belly of a perch or other panfish, and cooked or raw corn kernels.

HOMEMADE BAITS   There are many homemade baits which catch a lot of panfish and other ordinary fish, though they rarely catch game fish. High on the list of these baits is dough balls. Many old-timers believe that they know of some secret flavoring, odor, or ingredient, which they add to their mixtures to make them irresistible to certain species of fish. These anglers are entitled to their beliefs!

Homemade baits are especially useful when worms and other natural baits are hard to find, and this happens fairly often. Making most of these mixtures hold together is often the most difficult part of the job. Different ways of making homemade baits stick together are used by different anglers. A little honey, sometimes diluted with water; condensed milk; and, especially, tiny pieces of cotton wool, cotton, or gauze are mixed in as binders with ingredients such as bread, flour, cornmeal, and even tough doughy mixtures.

Small cubes of a tough crust of bread, or rolled pellets of bread mixed with a binder, will attract most small fish and most panfish.

Almost any kind of dough ball is most acceptable to carp or catfish, as well as other species. Some fishermen perfume these dough balls with a little anise or other scent which they believe will attract fish. Dough balls are made in various ways and of many mixtures. A tough, sticky dough with a binder added, cut into small, bait-size chunks, is one sort of dough ball. Sometimes dough mixed with cotton wool, just moist enough to work, is used. Mixing cornmeal and flour in equal parts with just enough water to form a paste, then mixing in a little binder, is another form of dough ball. Tiny pieces of meat or ground meat can be added along with the binder in the cornmeal and flour mixture. Try mixing some nippy cheese with some flour and a little honey. Knead this mixture into bait-size morsels. Some cotton wool may be added as a binder, if necessary.

Artificial Lures

One reason for the popularity of artificial lures is the fact that good, man-made lures appear so natural and behave so well in the water that fish are easily fooled by them, provided the fisherman fishes them cleverly. There are hundreds of lures of all sorts, including animal lures such as frogs and mice; insect lures such as grasshoppers, crickets, flies, and bugs of every description; and fish lures, such as minnows, sardines, and many

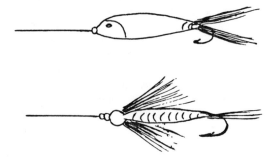

LURES

others. All of the best of these certainly deceive most fish. They are easy to come by, clean to handle, and do a good job.

Though many fish are smart and will size up a bait thoroughly before taking it, other fish are fooled by artificial lures and baits which appear, to human eyes, to look like nothing edible. Big fish and little ones too can be caught on hooks baited with small pieces of cloth, torn from a red and white handkerchief, or a small piece of sacking. Fish can also be taken on hooks baited with tinfoil, varicolored beads, short lengths of shoe laces, string, white tape, little bunches of varicolored wool taken from socks, red and white rose petals, morsels of nut husks, and shiny shells. Try to invent a lure.

SPOONS   About five thousand years ago, boys were fishing with a type of fish lure made from shells or pieces of shell or bone. Today, these artificial lures are known as spoons, and there are dozens of effective ones. Some are made of nickel, bright as spun silver; others are rich copper, brass, or gold in color, while many more are enameled in multi-colors. Spoons colored red and white are very effective. Some lures are also decorated with feathers.

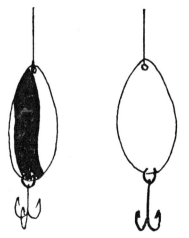

SPOONS

Even when full of food, trout and other game fish will often strike savagely at a lure which, by "swimming" and splashing all around the fish's home time after time, makes the fish angry. Some lures weigh from half an ounce on up and measure from under an inch to three inches and more.

Lures of this sort are made to operate at different levels. Some are surface-running lures, some float a little and run just an inch or two under the surface, while other lures run deep, going down after the big fellows which live and feed near or on the bottom. (See Chapter 6 for tips on manipulating lures.)

Many so-called weedless lures are not yet perfect, since they still manage to get snagged in weeds or lily pads, but they are useful when fishing weedy or lily pad-infested areas.

Many experienced fishermen hook about 2 inches of white pork rind, cut in a forked or streamer shape about 1/2 to 3/4 inch wide, onto spoons and similar lures. Such lures are considered an additional attraction for many kinds of fish.

PLUGS These lures are usually made of plastic or wood and are cleverly constructed to look like minnows, mice, frogs, and the like. Those weighing about half an ounce to one ounce serve best when used on a bait-casting rod. Some of these lures

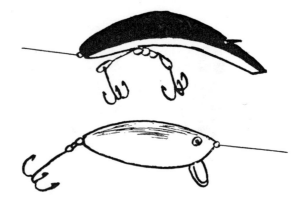

PLUGS

are surface plugs made to float, while others travel at various distances under water. The depth at which they travel is largely controlled by the manner in which they are fished.

There are many sorts of these surface lures and some of them are very effective, especially for largemouth bass. Some plugs which make loud popping noises are fish-getters, especially when surface fishing for black bass.

Fishing Safety

Fishing is fun, but all anglers have to watch out for their own safety and the safety of others. Be sure to follow the following rules:

- Learn to swim before you learn to fish.
- In a boat, always have a life preserver handy, just in case.
- Never carry fishing lines with hooks or plugs attached.
- Never fish close to other anglers unless forced to do so, as when in a boat.
- Never cast your line without being certain that there is nobody behind you or close enough to be hooked.
- Never wade in a lake, river, or any other fishing water without carefully testing each step in advance. Even small pools often have underwater shelves or other dropoffs where the water is unexpectedly deep.
- Never trust standing on flat underwater rocks or big stones without testing them with your foot. They are usually slippery.
- Never move around in or rock a small boat, especially one in which anyone is fishing.
- Never fish when a storm threatens. Lightning is especially dangerous when you are in a boat, or when you use a metal fishing rod.
- Always handle *any* hook with great care.
- Always use extra special care when handling bait casting plugs or spoons that contain clusters of double or triple hooks.
- Always be very careful when taking lures and hooks from the

water, especially snagged ones. A rod can whip these lures toward you or someone else close by with the speed of a bullet and can inflict nasty wounds or cause the loss of an eye.

First Aid For Fishermen

Before going fishing, a fellow should know what to do in case of accidents which occur on fishing trips. Many of the injuries met with are the same as those which happen to any outdoorsman. They usually happen on the way to or from favorite fishing spots, especially when the fisherman has to cross rough and thickly wooded country to reach these places. Falls resulting in bruises, cuts, and sprained ankles cause most of the damage.

Everybody who goes fishing should read a good first aid manual or at least the parts of it which deal with outdoor accidents and injuries. Some of these books come in pocket sizes. Treatment for a few of the most common injuries is given here.

BRUISES These are best treated by applying cold, *clean* water, when the skin is broken. Bruises usually take care of themselves, but sometimes rubbing them with a good liniment relieves the pain and helps to get rid of them faster.

CUTS Too often, careless fishermen cut themselves with a knife used for cutting bait and other things. Such cuts can be more dangerous than the average ones which happen outdoors because quite often the hands of a fisherman have been handling earth, earthworms, and the like, so the cuts can become easily infected.

The first treatment for a minor cut is to let it bleed a little. Sponge it with boiled water and antiseptic soap, then with an antiseptic solution, such as 3% hydrogen peroxide, to cleanse it. Place a small sterile pad on the wound; then bandage it with a clean bandage, a clean piece of cloth, or a clean handkerchief. After the fishing trip, the wound or cut should be examined, washed again with an antiseptic solution, if necessary, and bandaged again. If there is swelling or pus caused by infection forming in such an injury, let a doctor look at it.

DROWNING   This is one of the great hazards facing fishermen. Drowning can result from slipping on underwater stones and rocks, which offer only dangerous footing; falling from a slippery log or jetty, or the sudden collapse of an overhanging bank on the edge of a stream. Drowning can also occur very easily from any boat used for fishing. Sometimes a small boat will overturn because of carelessness on the part of even one occupant, or from the wash of a bigger boat, caused by careless navigation on the part of one or both boatmen. The majority of accidents are needless and can be avoided by using common sense, care, and presence of mind.

Because of the danger of drowning, boys should learn to swim before fishing anywhere. On any fishing craft, a sufficient number of life belts, kept handy, will help to save lives. A long pole or a length of stout rope can also be lifesavers when fishermen fall from banks, logs, or piers into deep or even shallow water. Many people are drowned in only a foot or so of water!

Everyone who goes fishing should have a fair knowledge of artificial respiration. The Schafer (back pressure) and Holger Nielsen (back pressure and arms lift) methods are approved by various lifesaving societies. There is also the mouth-to-mouth method of resuscitation, which can best be given by use of an air tube, known as an airway. These methods of saving life are fully explained in good first aid and/or lifesaving manuals.

FISH HOOK INJURIES   Injuries caused by fish hooks, especially ones from treble hook groups, are among the wounds which are most difficult to treat because the barbs, embedded perhaps deeply under the skin, must be removed before the wound can be treated against infection. Even when a single hook has penetrated a fingertip, the correct way to remove the barb is to push the hook on through the finger and snip the barb off with a pair of wire snips. This is a minor operation but a very painful one to the victim. This sort of treatment should only be given by a grownup who has a knowledge of first aid, or, better still, a doctor. Once the hook has been removed, the cut should be allowed to bleed a little, then sponged with an antiseptic solution and bandaged with a clean bandage.

Not only can fishermen injure themselves with these dangerous weapons but they can, even more easily, wound a fishing companion. Fortunately, wounds of this sort never need occur when fishermen use common sense and great care in handling and using fish hooks of any sort.

SPRAINS   A sprained finger, wrist, or ankle can best be treated by applying cold, wet cloths, or by placing the injured part in cold water, then bandaging it fairly tightly. Afterwards, as in the case of bruises, the injured part may be rubbed with a good liniment to relieve pain and help healing.

FIRST AID KIT   Only a few first aid items need be taken along for the use of a lone fisherman. A few necessary things, such as those listed below, should be packed in a small, waterproof box.

band-aids, assorted sizes
adhesive tape, assorted widths, medicated and waterproof
gauze bandages, assorted sizes
sterile pads and dressings, assorted sizes
small pair of scissors

a few small safety pins
a small cake of medicated soap
hydrogen peroxide, 3% solution (antiseptic for wounds)
insect repellent
sunburn lotion

CHAPTER 6

Going Fishing

THERE ARE MANY ways to fish, but three basic methods are generally used. Still-fishing, bait casting, and trolling.

Still-fishing

This is also known as drop line fishing, especially when it is used to fish from the banks of streams, bridges, causeways, piers, docks, floats, and boats. It is perhaps the easiest and least expensive form of angling, as it requires only a length of line, held in the hand, a hook, sinker, and bait. It is an exciting way to fish because every time a fish even samples the bait it is communicated directly through the line to the hand which holds it. More panfish are caught by this easy method than by all other ways of fishing combined.

Still-fishing is a waiting game which can be enjoyed by fishermen in almost all waters, fresh or salt. Besides the minimum gear listed above, one can add a bobber, a fishing pole or an inexpensive fishing rod, and a leader to the end of the line. These do add somewhat to the sport and fun, though one can get along quite nicely without them. One advantage of a reel is that it allows the sport of playing a fish, instead of just yanking it onto the bank or dock.

Nobody can tell a fellow just how deep to fish his bait in order to catch the most fish in this method of fishing. Different kinds of fish, different waters, and the temperature of the water require that the bait be kept either on the bottom or at various depths, in order to take fish. When one is after fish which feed on the bottom, there is no problem. With other species it is an easy matter to try the bait at different depths until the right one is found. A bobber, working in partnership with a sinker of the right weight, will keep the bait at the right depth, where fish may be caught.

Many skillful fishermen have graduated from still-fishing to bait casting, trolling, spinning, and dry fly fishing, in that order, but there is nothing to prevent a boy from learning spin fishing before he has learned to use a standard bait casting rod.

Bait Casting

This is an easier way of fishing than spinning or fly casting. One can bait cast from a shoreline, dock, bridge, or causeway in either fresh or salt water. A rod about 5 feet long or a little longer is needed. A reel is the most important part of bait casting gear. For a start, about 30 to 50 yards of good-quality nylon or linen line, ranging from 8- to 12-pound test is needed. A light line for smaller fish, especially when you are using a lightweight lure, is best in streams or lakes which are comparatively snag-free. In waters which are weed- or lily pad-infested, and when a heavy plug is on the line, a heavier line is needed. The size of the hook, for natural bait or lures of different sizes, is decided to a large degree by the size of the fish being sought. When using natural bait or a light lure, a sinker may also be used. A 2- or 3-inch spoon, with single or treble hooks, fishes well from a bait casting rod.

The combination of rod and reel makes it possible to make long casts from a bank or boat and to direct the bait into the area which you wish to fish. Though bait casting may seem as easy as projecting a ball of clay from the end of a throwing stick, it is not nearly as simple as that. Accuracy is often as important as distance in casting.

Here are a few pointers for beginners: Hold the rod with the reel crank upward, four fingers around the rod and with the thumb (which controls the action of the reel) pressing half on the line and half on the side of the spool. Let a short length of line, around 3 inches for a heavy lure and 9 inches for a light lure, hang from the tip of the rod. Raise the rod tip upward, using wrist action, until the rod is vertical (fishermen call this the twelve o'clock position, because the tip of the rod points to twelve o'clock). Now snap the rod downward fast, using hand and wrist, releasing the thumb pressure to let the line run out, then thumbing again to stop the lure above your target.

Marvelous reels can be bought with all sorts of automatic controls which do practically all of the work, but such reels cost a lot of money and spoil part of the fun and personal skill which makes fishing fascinating. A most important point in using the reel is to learn to handle it so that backlash and snarls do not happen.

The best way to become a good bait caster is to practice a lot, at different ranges, and with different weights taking the place of lures and sinkers. Watching skillful bait casters in action is also helpful.

Trolling

The best way to troll—that is, to make your bait or lure travel through the water so that fish will strike at it at different depths—is from behind a boat. Pulling baited line through the water while walking along a jetty or a river bank is a form of trolling. Trolling may be done with a rod or handline on the surface of the water, at medium depth, or deep down, depending on the kind of fish which you hope to catch and the waters that you troll. Trolling may be done from a rowboat or a boat driven by an outboard or inboard motor.

To troll, a short, rather stout rod or boat rod and a fairly heavy line are best. Many experienced fishermen prefer to troll with artificial lures, such as spoons or plugs. These are easier to find and use than live or natural baits, which range from whole small fish to shellfish and pork rind.

Trolling by hand from behind a boat provides the thrill of a strike that never comes from trolling with a rod. Trolling may be done by fishing directly behind the boat or by trolling over the side. When trolling on dull days, or when the water is murky or inclined to be rough, a short length of line, say 20 to 30 feet, is best. On clear days, and on calm waters, a longer line, 30 to 60 feet, may be used to advantage. Longer lines are also better, as a rule, when trolling behind a boat driven by an outboard motor.

When trolling from a rowboat, it should be rowed in a rather slow, steady manner. Any noise made in the boat such as scuffing the feet on the floorboards or setting the tackle box down noisily, will scare fish away. On salt water, especially when fishing close to shore, rowing in a zigzag manner will sometimes get good results, not only because some fish, such as striped bass, often feed inshore, but also because the zigzag method covers more water. Approach fish which are feeding near the shore from the deep water side.

From a rowboat, start by letting out 25 to 35 feet of line. If necessary, one can let out as much as 75 feet. Reels should be fixed at these distances so that more line will not run out. Lure action will be given by the boat movement.

When trolling alone from a boat, one can fish with the butt end of the rod fastened in some way to a fairly heavy stone, the floorboard, or the thwart. A simple way, when using a line with or without a rod, is to wind a part of the line a few times around a flat stone, placed in the bottom of the boat at the stern. The weight of the stone will usually set the hook and give you time to reach the line and take over.

Fishing Pointers

The following pointers on fishing can easily make the difference between a good catch and a very poor one.

- Start off with the best fishing gear you can afford for the sort of fishing you intend to do.
- Keep fish hooks sharp. A piece of carborundum for sharpening fish hooks is a must for all fishermen.
- Use a small hook in preference to a big one. A big hook will rarely catch a small fish, but a small hook will often catch a big fish.
- Soak spinners, spoons, and other metal lures for a while in water in which potatoes have been boiled. This will make them gleam and glisten.
- When fishing at sea or on a lake, keep an eye open for gulls and other water birds which are fish eaters. Where they gather, the fish are.
- Don't let cold hands spoil the fun of spring and fall fishing. Cold hands can become raw through exposure to wind and water. To prevent this, take along a small plastic bottle filled with olive oil. Rub the oil thoroughly into the hands and wrists. This keeps wind and water from making direct contact with the skin. A little olive oil rubbed into the face will prevent windburn and will help to keep the sun at bay, too.
- Always net a hooked fish which has been played until it is tired and brought alongside a boat or dock, in the water. Guide it into the net head first, making sure that no part of the fish touches the rim of the net while being netted. When no landing net is handy, always seize the fish behind the gills, so that it will not slip out of your hand. A piece of thin cloth, even a handkerchief, will make landing the fish easier.
- Make soft baits of almost any sort fast to a hook by tying them onto it with a short length of lightweight, strong nylon thread.
- When baiting a hook with a worm, place the worm on the ground and watch in which direction it heads. Hook about half an inch below this end and thread the worm onto the hook, leaving a short end—about half an inch—just below the barb, to wiggle and attract fish. It is easier to thread a worm onto a long-shanked hook.
- Use lily pad bait if you run out of worms. Sometimes a worm may be found by splitting the stalk of a lily pad which has a

hole in its center.

- Carry a stout staff, about four or five feet long, to press against the bed of the stream for balance and to probe for deep spots, when wading a stream or fishing along the edges of a river. A loop of cord can keep it on the wrist, or a short length of cord can secure it to the belt, so that it will not float away when you are playing a fish.

GETTING ACTION FROM LURES   Much of the fun of fishing consists of uncertainty about where the fish are to be found and where they may be feeding, and trying to guess their favorite food for the day. An experienced fisherman may take along a dozen different kinds of artificial baits, ranging from brightly colored lures to frogs and flies, in the hope of outwitting wary fish who are rather fussy about what they will eat on that particular kind of day. Being able to catch fish in this way is the mark of a true fisherman.

Depending on fishing conditions, there are special ways of getting fish with spoons and similar lures which are drawn through the water. Whether fishing is done from the banks of a lake or stream or from a boat, some days the fish will strike lures which are drawn rather quickly through the water. Other fish will hit at slow-moving lures, while still others find great appeal in a lure which swims along with a fast, slow, fast, slow rhythm. Some fish will take a spoon when it is floating on the surface, and this is a thrilling sight. Other fish will strike when the lure is deep down, and only their savage tug on the line indicates a strike and a possible catch. These are a few of the things which an amateur fisherman must learn before he can be classed as a real fish-taker. Much of the art and skill of fishing may be learned from fishing companions who know the waters and the best bait for the sorts of fish that live there, but a great deal also may be learned by the lone, amateur fisherman who finds out for himself, usually through trial-and-error methods, just how to fish for fun and sport. This is where the top thrills of fishing are to be found.

WHERE TO CATCH FISH   The question most often asked

by novice fishermen is where to catch fish. Answers vary, depending on what kind of water is to be fished, what the fisherman hopes to catch, the bait used, and whether the fish being sought live in the waters being fished. Catching fish also depends to some extent on water temperature and weather conditions—whether the day is cloudy, hot, or cool, and the direction in which the wind is blowing.

Boys who hope to catch catfish and panfish in general during the day should know that most of these fish feed on the bottom and in schools. It's foolish to try for these fish just under or on the surface, since unless the water is quite shallow, none of these species are likely to be caught, even though you may be within yards of them.

Panfish are the kind which beginning fishermen most often go after. It is fun catching them and, when a number have been caught, they make an excellent fish fry. Sunfish, including the bluegills, form part of the panfish family. Bluegills and perch

SUNFISH

are not only tasty but they also put up a good fight, especially the bluegills, when hooked on light tackle. Crappies, also known as calico bass; rock, white, and yellow bass; and yellow perch are all in the panfish class. Though small—averaging around five or six inches—they are tasty morsels.

PERCH

Here are some likely places to catch most sorts of fish:

- Where the water foams and whirls at the foot of a waterfall or in a stream or river. Game fish gather in search of food in such places.
- Under or at the edge of banks of rivers and streams.
- Behind, around, or under logs or big rocks and in deep holes, often the favorite haunts of some big fellows.
- Under lily pads and in small pockets between patches of lily pads.
- Around pilings, piers, stumps, and the like.
- Over submerged sand bars, above wreckage, and around rocks, points, and peninsulas.

Once you have found out the most likely places to fish in a pond, lake, or stream, you are well on your way. Just why many fish like certain parts of ponds, lakes, or streams best is hard for even experienced fishermen to tell. Nevertheless, the experts do find out by fishing these waters, and their information is passed on or found out so that in time less expert fishermen find these spots also. The sorts of bait which are used to catch fish are also soon known to the fishermen of a village or town. It is a big thrill for a boy who is an amateur fisherman to make a good catch by using baits and fishing spots different from those of the experts, and this often happens.

WHEN TO CHANGE FISHING STRATEGY   It has already been pointed out that patience is one of the first things needed to become a really good fisherman. Though this is true, it does not mean that one should fish the same spot hour after hour without getting at least a few encouraging nibbles. The thing to do in such cases is to move around the lake a bit, or up and down the stream a little until you do get results. Probably food supply, temperature of the water, or other things are causing the fish to gather in certain spots on a particular morning or afternoon. Tomorrow, things may change again.

Patience does not mean fishing the same bait or lure which is not getting results, hour after hour. A good fisherman changes his lure after trying it for a reasonable time. Perhaps, if the day is cloudy or the water a little murky, it requires a brighter lure to attract fish. Again, the fish may be feeding a little deeper than usual or closer to the surface, which often happens, except in the case of fish which are known to be ground feeders. Perhaps, after fishing down deep for a reasonable while, you should try skittering a surface lure over the water where you believe fish are to be found. You will have to think of ways to outwit the fish who are, apparently, not to be had that morning.

Once the fish begin to take the bait, things surely pick up, but even then a fellow must not let the sudden change make him careless about catching the fish. Some fish need to be allowed to sample the bait a little, especially live bait, before deciding to eat it. After that, it is time to set the hook with a slight, sharp wrist movement, not a sharp yank that pulls the bait out of the fish's mouth.

PLAYING THE FISH   Once a fish is hooked, play him as well as you know how. The chief thing is to tire him so that he may be brought to hand or net easily and surely. Keeping the rod tip low while keeping the fish on the move is one way to do this. No sporting fisherman will use a heavy rod and line and simply haul his fish ashore, once it is securely hooked. When using light rod, line, and tackle, even the smaller fish have to be played skillfully in order to land them. This is where fishing fun and know-how come in.

For boys who learn and develop through practice many fishing ways, fishing as a hobby will always have something new to offer in the way of thrill and sport.

CHAPTER **7**

Strange
Flying
Things

EVEN A BOY who doesn't know much about aerodynamics
will begin to understand what air pressures and thermals of
various sorts are and what they can do, after he invents a few
flying objects. Thermals are hot or warm currents of air rising
up from the ground. Big thermals, such as those rising up from
a valley, have great lifting power, but even the smallest thermal
stream will carry lightweight, flat-surfaced flying objects, such
as the flying saucer and the frog described in this chapter
rapidly upward. It is much easier to let such flying things locate
a thermal, in the course of their flight, rather than try to locate
a thermal in advance by tossing small pieces of tissue paper into
the air.

How to Estimate Wind Velocity

All flying objects, including kites, should be flown with the
flier's back to the wind. It is well to know something of the wind
forces. Since even a good, lightweight kite, flown on a light but

strong line, should fly in a 4-mile-per-hour breeze, the lighter fliers described in this chapter require very little in the way of breeze and thermals to take them up.

THE BEAUFORT SCALE   The Beaufort scale of wind force classifies wind speeds. A knowledge of it is helpful in estimating wind velocity. Here are some of the Beaufort classifications, which apply to wind speeds at 30 feet above ground:

Beaufort Number	Miles per Hour	Description
0	Less than 1	Calm: air quite still, smoke rises straight up.
1	1 to 3	Light air: weather vanes do not move but smoke drifts.
2	4 to 7	Light breeze: weather vanes move, wind is felt on face, and leaves rustle.
3	8 to 12	Gentle breeze: wind extends light flags, leaves and branches move.
4	13 to 18	Moderate to still breeze: wind blows dust and loose paper about and small branches are in motion.

The numbers continue to increase as the wind rises, but the above indications are useful for small flying objects and small and medium-size kites.

Many boys have invented and flown flying objects of such weird appearance that most of them could have been placed in the U.F.O. category. Of course, a little experimenting is a big part of the fun of flying unusual things.

After learning something about balance by experimenting in building and flying such objects, it is not difficult to construct strange flying things of various sizes and made from different materials. Have a try!

Among the things which can be flown are lightweight paper bags, with the top edges folded and pasted together, and an oblong or oval about 3 inches wide and 6 to 10 inches long (depending on the size of the paper bag), cut in one side. A few strips of stiff paper, pasted on where necessary, help to keep the bag in shape. With the addition of one or two light tails, suspended from the middle or each end, the object is ready to take off. A lightweight but strong thread or twine attached to each side of the opening is used to fly the thing.

Flexible Fliers

Non-rigid objects, such as parachutes made from strong tissue paper or lightweight cloth, will fly with the addition of

PARACHUTE-TYPE FLIER

lightweight cords or threads each about 12 to 18 inches long. About six or eight of them are attached to the edges of the object and tied off on a small, lightweight plastic ring, which hangs beneath the object. This parachute-type flier requires a lightweight tail, sewn or fastened by string onto one side of the object. A light flying line is attached to the ring. If well-made, the parachute will take off very well. One advantage of non-rigid flying things is that they are almost indestructible.

The Flying Saucer

This very effective circular flying object is not difficult to make. It may be made in various sizes, from 8 to 10 inches in diameter to considerably larger, from a sheet of strong, stiff, lightweight paper. You will also need three strips of basswood or balsa (often sold in hobby supply stores), about 3/8 inch wide for smaller models and about 1/2 inch wide for larger ones, cut to the lengths required. These are pasted onto the saucer to reinforce it. A piece of strong, stiff paper is also needed for making the keel. The length and width of this paper depends on the size of the saucer.

Let's say that you decide to make a saucer 10 inches in diameter. Trace a circle 10 inches in diameter onto a sheet of newspaper with a compass or, if necessary, draw around a 10-inch plate, to make a pattern. Place a ruler across the circle so that its edge intersects the diameter at a point about 3 inches inside the rim; then draw a line across the circle. (About a third of the diameter of the circle will lie between the line and the circumference of the circle.) This line is line 1 in the drawing. Again using a ruler, draw another line across the opposite end of the circle so that it intersects the diameter at a point about 1 inch from the rim. This is line 2 in the drawing. Now, measuring 3 inches from line 2, draw line 3 between lines 1 and 2, as shown. To make sure that all the lines are parallel, line up the end of the ruler with the edge of the paper when drawing the lines. These lines show where the basswood strips are to be pasted on the real saucer.

Cut the pattern carefully along the outline; then fold it in half, seeing that lines 1, 2, and 3 meet at each side, and make a center fold all the way from end to end along the exact center of the pattern, as shown by the broken line in step 3 of the illustration. This will indicate where the keel is to be pasted later. Trim along the line that runs 1 inch from the outer edge of the saucer, from side to side. This squared-off end will be the front end of the saucer.

Now, place the pattern onto strong, lightweight paper. Trace the outline and draw the lines on it the same as they are on the

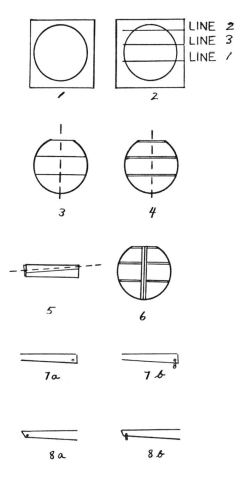

LINE 2
LINE 3
LINE /

STEPS IN MAKING THE FLYING SAUCER

(1) Trace circle onto sheet of newspaper, to make a pattern. (2) Draw lines across circle to show where basswood strips will be pasted on saucer. (3) Cut out circle, make center fold to show where keel will be pasted, and trim along line 2. (4) Trace around pattern onto stiff paper, draw lines, cut around outline, and paste on basswood strips. (5) Fold keel, draw lines as shown (be sure to draw the lower line on each side), cut along outer (broken) line, and paste keel together from fold to lower lines. (6) Paste flaps of keel onto saucer. (7a) Punch hole through keel for tail attachment. (7b) Thread string through hole and fasten to ring. (8a) Trim keel in front as shown and punch hole in keel for flying line attachment. (8b) Thread string through hole and fasten to ring.

pattern. Also draw a line corresponding to the center fold of the pattern. Cut around the outline. Paste or cement a strip of basswood along the edge which has been trimmed; then paste a strip along each of the two lines, as in step 4. Now the saucer is ready for a keel.

Make the keel from a piece of stiff, strong paper, 9 or 10 inches long by 6 inches wide. (A smaller saucer requires a shorter and narrower keel, and a larger saucer needs a longer and wider one. The keel must always be as long as the saucer.) Fold the paper lengthwise exactly down the center, and turn the folded side toward you. From the fold, measure up 1 inch at the left end and 1 3/4 inch at the right. Draw a straight line from one mark to the other; then draw another line 3/4 inch above it, as indicated by the broken line in step 5. Cut carefully along this outer (broken) line. Turn the keel over and draw the same inner line on that side. Now, fold the keel carefully along the lines on each side. The 3/4-inch flaps on each side are what you use to paste the keel onto the saucer, but first paste the keel together along its entire length, from the fold to the lines only. Be careful not to get any paste onto the flaps. When the paste is thoroughly dry, paste the keel along the entire length of the saucer, where the center line is marked. The small (1-inch) end belongs at the front end of the saucer and the wide end at the rear. Be sure that the center of the keel (where the two flaps of the keel fold over) is on the exact center of the saucer. The 3/4-inch flap on each side of the keel, in addition to holding the keel in position, as shown in step 6, helps to reinforce the saucer from end to end, as do the wooden strips from side to side.

Now the saucer is ready for the attachments of a tail and a flying line.

TAIL ATTACHMENT This is how the keel is prepared for the tail attachment. With an ice pick or awl punch a small hole through the keel, about 1/2 inch from the foot and 1/2 inch from its rear end, as in step 7a. Reinforce the hole with a small gummed reinforcement circle, one on each side. If there are none handy, make your own from a piece of tough paper and paste them on. Thread a short piece of thin string through the hole and fasten it to a small, lightweight ring about 3/16 inch or 1/4 inch in diameter, so that the ring hangs about 3/8 inch below the keel, as in step 7b. A square knot (see Chapter 5) may be used. The string tail will be threaded through this ring and fastened to it.

FLYING LINE ATTACHMENT   The flying line attachment is made in the same way as the tail attachment, except that the keel should be trimmed about 1/2 inch in front, at an angle, as in step 8a. Then the hole is punched 3/4 inch from this end and reinforced. A short piece of string is threaded through this hole and fastened to a lightweight ring the same size as the one used for the tail attachment, as in step 8b. This ring, too, should hang about 3/8 inch below the keel.

TAIL   The flying saucer needs a string tail to stabilize it. The length of the tail and its weight will depend on the size of the saucer and the conditions under which it is flown. These vary from day to day, so it is wise to take along extra string. It is easy to shorten or add to the string tail. From 12 to 30 feet of ordinary thin twine should do for smaller saucers. If heavier twine is used, the tail can be shorter, but at least 15 feet is best to assure stability and graceful flying qualities.

FLYING LINE   The flying saucer may be flown on a very light piece of twine or string, since its action is a gliding and soaring one, which exerts little pull on the line. Crochet thread

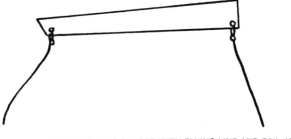

KEEL OF FLYING SAUCER WITH FLYING LINE AND TAIL ATTACHED

is also satisfactory. A spool or reel is useful to prevent the line tangling (see Lines and Reels in Chapter 8). The greatest strain on the flying line is the jerk given when the line is used to give the saucer free flight by remote control, described below under Hand Line Releases.

Hand Line Releases

Releases of various sorts can be used to release different things from the saucer and other flying objects described in this chapter, as well as from bridles, fly cords, and tails of kites. The hand line release which follows is also ideal for boys who fly gliders. This simple hand line release, invented by the author, is quite effective, whether used as a single or dual release device.

Such a device can be used as a double release, to remove the tail by remote control from the flying saucer and, at the same instant, release the saucer from its flying line, so that it can float free. Benefiting from a fast-rising thermal, one of these flying saucers flew free over the skyscrapers of New York City until lost to view of binoculars.

SINGLE RELEASE   To make the simplest, single form, of this release, you will need one strong, medium-sized, metal hairpin about 2 inches long. A crimped hairpin works best. Snip off the two ends of the hairpin, leaving about 3/4 inch of shank on each side at the top, and you have the release. The lightweight line on which you fly the saucer is tied securely to the curve on the top of the hairpin, instead of being tied directly to the ring hanging from the keel.

To attach the release, simply pull the two ends of the hairpin apart a little, to make a spring. Remember that the farther they are pulled apart, the stronger the spring will be. Now, pinch the ends toward each other for a moment and push them through the ring hanging below the keel, in front, with the head of the hairpin hanging downward.

A sharp jerk on the flying line will cause the two ends of the hairpin to pull through the ring, leaving the saucer to soar in free flight. However, before it can glide and soar well, the tail also must be removed.

DUAL RELEASE This is made with exactly the same simple gadget, a hairpin, cut in the same way as the one which is used on the flying line. The top end of the flying saucer tail string is fastened to the curved end of the hairpin spring. The two ends of this spring are pulled apart slightly, so that they will remain in position during the flight, after they have been pushed through the small ring suspended below the keel at the rear of the saucer.

To complete the dual release control, a length of strong, thin string or heavy cotton thread is attached between the flying cord and the tail string. The short length of string should be attached by one end directly below the head of the hairpin on the flying line. The other end is fastened directly below the hairpin head on the tail string. This connecting string must be long enough to allow about 1 inch of slack when attached. A little experimenting will show that this allows enough play to adapt to the angle of the hairpin when the flying cord pulls on it and the tail trails slightly behind when in flight. If the con-

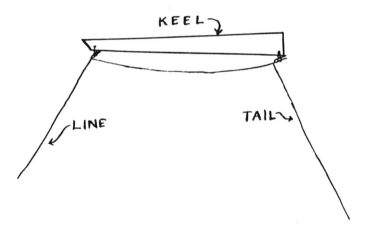

DUAL HAND LINE RELEASE

necting line is too taut, it will pull the hairpin out before you are ready to send the saucer into free flight. On the other hand, if it is too long, it will not operate instantaneously, as it will if it is the right length. When the connecting line is the correct length, one gentle but sharp tug—two, if necessary—on the flying line will release both the flying line and the tail, allowing the saucer to float and glide in entirely free flight.

Of course, the hairpins can be used in pairs, or in groups of threes, to increase the resistance against wind pull, or when larger flying saucers are made and flown.

The author hopes that this little invention will open doors of thought and experimentation by the readers of this book.

The Flying Frog

This is a very effective flying thing which the author invented. It flies with its long hind legs dangling behind it. They act as stabilizers as the frog soars and flies on an even keel, without a tail. The frog can be made as follows:

First, make a pattern from stiff paper or thin cardboard about 11 inches long by 8 1/2 inches wide, drawing the frog on it, as in step 1 of the illustration. Draw a line exactly down the center from end to end, to indicate where the keel is to go, as shown by the broken line in step 2 of the drawing. Be sure that the frog is as fat on one side of that center line as on the other, so it will balance well in flight. When you are satisfied with your drawing, cut the pattern out carefully. Place the pattern on a sheet of stiff, lightweight paper and trace around it; then cut carefully along the edge. Paste a strip of thick paper or thin cardboard 3/8 inch wide along the frog's chin, as in step 2.

The next important step is to make the keel from a piece of stiff paper 11 inches long by 6 inches wide. It is made in the same way as the keel for the flying saucer (see above), except that it is an inch longer. Paste the keel along the exact center of the frog, from tip of nose to end, with the narrow end of the keel at the nose.

The frog's legs are made from strips of tissue paper, or similar lightweight paper. The legs are pasted onto the body of the frog.

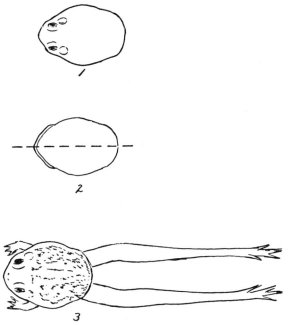

STEPS IN MAKING THE FLYING FROG

(1) Draw a pattern as shown. (2) After tracing around pattern onto stiff paper and cutting around outline, paste strip of paper or cardboard along frog's chin, as shown. (3) Completed frog.

Two short legs, each 6 to 8 inches long are pasted one at each side of the head. The hind legs, each about 36 inches long, are pasted one on each side at the back end. Since these stabilizing legs take the place of a tail, their length will change with flying conditions, so some extra inches may have to be pasted onto the end of each leg or, perhaps, a few inches may have to be cut off, so that the balance of the frog in flight is correct. It will vary with the breeze and thermals.

A small, lightweight ring about 3/16 to 1/4 inch in diameter is suspended from a small hole made in the front end of the keel, about 1/2 inch from the keel, which is trimmed and prepared in the same way as the keel for the flying saucer. The flying line is also attached in the same way.

Boomerangs

Boomerangs are interesting flying things. They have been used all over the world for hunting, warfare, and fun. The throwing stick of the Pueblo Indians of the Southwest is one form of boomerang, though when it misses it does not return to

AUSTRALIAN BOOMERANG

or close to the thrower. It is not difficult to make boomerangs of various sorts and shapes. They can be painted in two or more colors, so that they look fine as they glide and circle and can be found more easily when they land.

The kind of wood used in making any flying thing is important. It should be straight-grained, lightweight, and strong. Among the most suitable woods are basswood, tulip (white-wood), and pine. The usual thickness of the strips used is 1/8 inch and 1/4 inch. The size of wings and suggested dimensions are given for each type described.

The ends of the wing sections of all boomerangs must be curved slightly upward. Regardless of size, the bending point of the wings should be two-thirds of the distance from end to center.

The two edges of each stick or wing are slightly beveled on one side, to give a cutting edge as the boomerang is thrown into the air. About 1 inch of each is not beveled, at the ends, in order to make the ends stronger for landing. The beveling can be done easily with a piece of sandpaper.

For the sake of visibility, the stripes painted on boomerangs should be bright red, blue, green, or black. The background color should be a light one, such as aluminum, white, or pale yellow. Several colors can be used on a boomerang, but all the wings should be painted exactly alike in order to look well in flight.

Lightweight metal bolts of suitable lengths and thicknesses, threaded from top to end and fitted with a wing nut, are the best means of fastening the wings together in all boomerangs. The wing nuts can be loosened easily, to fold the wings together when the boomerang is not being used, and a few twists on the nut will hold the wings firmly in position, to make it ready for flight.

Here are a few easy-to-make boomerangs. How they are made and what they look like when completed is shown in the drawings. Suggested dimensions are given, but the boomerangs may be made in various sizes.

SQUARE BOOMERANG   In this model, each stick is 20

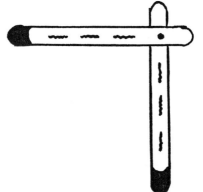

SQUARE BOOMERANG

inches long, 1 or 1 1/4 inches wide, and 1/8 inch thick. The sticks overlap 2 inches, where bolted together.

TWO-WING BOOMERANG   The sticks used in this type

TWO-WING BOOMERANG

of boomerang are from 18 to 24 inches long, 1 1/4 or 1 1/2 inches in width, and 1/8 inch thick. The ends are cut as shown in the drawing.

THREE-WING PINWHEEL-TYPE BOOMERANG Though this is an easy model to make, it looks equally fine in and out of flight. The sticks can be 24 inches long, 2 inches wide at

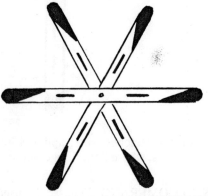

THREE-WING PINWHEEL-TYPE BOOMERANG

the ends, and 1 1/2 inches wide at the center of the boomerang. The thickness of the wood may be 1/8 inch or 3/16 inch. The wing nut, at the back of the model, holds the sticks together.

This model can be made in different ways. For instance, the sticks may be 1 1/2 inches wide from end to end and 20 to 30 inches long, the thickness of the wood being 1/8 inch.

THREE-WING CONVERTIBLE MODEL   The three-wing convertible model can easily be converted into the three-wing fan-type boomerang. Both types fly equally well. The wings of the convertible model can be 18 inches long, 2 1/2 inches wide

THREE-WING CONVERTIBLE BOOMERANG

with tapered ends, and 1 1/2 inches wide at the center of the boomerang. The wood is 1/8 inch thick. The sticks form a near-"Y."

THREE-WING FAN-TYPE BOOMERANG   This model is exactly the same as the one shown above. It is made by loosening the wing nut behind the wings, adjusting them to the form of a fan, and then tightening the nut.

THREE-WING FAN-TYPE BOOMERANG

Once a few boomerangs have been made and flown successfully, it is interesting to dream up models of various types and sizes and experiment to see which color schemes show up best in flight.

THROWING A BOOMERANG   Throwing a boomerang well requires a good deal of practice and patience before it will swerve to left or right, circle, and glide back, landing fairly close to the thrower. A start may be made with a lightweight, square-type boomerang. Hold one wing lightly by the end, between the thumb and index finger, with the thumb used for balance. Heavier and larger boomerangs may be held with the end between the four fingers and the palm of the hand, with the end of the stick just touching the middle finger.

A boomerang may be thrown forward with the arm held nearly horizontally when the throw is made. It may also be thrown with the arm held vertically. Another good position is with the arm at an angle, halfway between the horizontal and vertical positions. A slight jerk may be used as the boomerang leaves the hand. Even boomerangs of the same style, built in the same way, and of the same size and weight, may fly in different manners, so a fellow has to note and learn the peculiarities of each one and how it may be flown best.

FLIGHT RECORD CHART   A chart may be kept to show just how each boomerang should be thrown to get the best results. They may be thrown for distance, height, and circling ability. The best throwing position of each boomerang may be noted and notations made indicating the flight faults of each. Some of the faults, not due to poor throws, may be corrected, and the flight range and style improved by studying the flight records.

Bull-Roarers

Bull-roarers are flown on the end of a line. These easily made noisemakers were used long ago in various ceremonies by North American Indian tribes and the aborigines of Australia, especially for bringing rain. The rainmakers used by these ancient Australians were made from heavy hardwood cut to a length of about 18 inches and a width of around 6 inches. These roarers were flat, the thickness ranging from about 1/8 inch to 1/2 inch. When whirled rapidly above the head or spun vertically from a strong thong or woven cord, which was the usual way of using them, they made a loud moaning sound which was believed to bring thunderstorms and rain.

The Hopi use a thong or cord which must be as long as the distance from the heart to the fingertips of the right hand when the arm is extended. A heavy cord, the Hopi say, will reduce the noise of the bull-roarer, so they prefer two thin, strong cords, tightly interwoven. Some of the medicine men were very clever at making bull-roarers out of various sorts of hardwood and notching them in certain ways, so that they really roared loudly.

A little practice with experimental bull-roarers made from some softwood, such as pine or spruce, which is easy to shape and work, will help you decide which sort of noisemaker works best. Then a copy of the most effective bull-roarer can be made from some hardwood which will not break easily, such as oak or ash. There are two quite different sorts of bull-roarers which you can make without difficulty. One sort can be made in this way:

Shape a flat piece of softwood about 8 inches long, 2 inches wide, and 1/4 inch thick, into an oval, as illustrated. Sandpaper the roarer after beveling the top side to a fairly sharp edge,

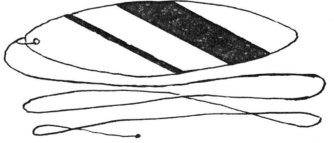

BULL-ROARER

STRANGE FLYING THINGS • 109

leaving the bottom flat. The bull-roarer may be painted some bright color and marked with stripes or circles in a darker color. Bore a small hole in the center of one end of the roarer, about 1/2 inch from the end. Fasten a thin, strong piece of twine or cord through the hole, either by tying a knot on the end of the string or by using a bowline knot (see Chapter 9). The bull-roarer should be swung quickly by holding the free end of the cord in one hand and swinging the roarer in a vertical circle.

The second type of bull-roarer is made from a flat piece of heavy wood, the same size as the one above. Except for an inch at the end, to which the cord is fastened, these noisemakers are serrated with "V"-shaped notches ranging from 1/8 inch to 3/8 inch deep, usually the same size notch being used through-

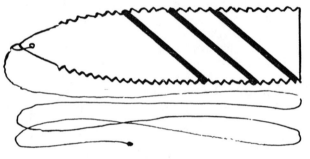

NOTCHED BULL-ROARER

out. Boys may experiment with the sizes and depths of notches in their roarers. The tail end of this type of roarer is not notched but is squared off. These roarers are not beveled as a rule.

A contest may be held to see who can have his roarer produce the loudest booming sound. Bull-roarers can really roar; they are used by the natives in Malaya to stampede elephants!

CHAPTER 8

Go
Fly A
Kite!

KITE-FLYING IS PROBABLY the most international of all sports. It is enjoyed by millions of boys and grownups alike. Nearly 30,000,000 kites of all sorts are sold in the United States each year. Although one can fight with kites and cut an opponent's kite down, kite-flying is really a friendly sport, as shown by the slogan of the International Kitefliers Association: "Worldwide Friends Through Kite-Flying."

Building a Kite

Building a good kite with perfect balance—one that rises, flies, reels in easily, and flies gracefully—takes some skill and patience. It is well to remember that even the best kite is a heavier-than-air machine. Some specialty kites take almost as long to make as a fine model airplane, but the result is worthwhile. The ordinary kite, say the diamond-shaped, 3-foot model, can be made in an hour or less, but such a kite is not likely to win any event in a kite-flying tournament. Experienced kite builders usually make blueprints of a proposed model, which can save hours in rebuilding, should the kite become lost.

It is often much easier to get a big kite, say a 6-foot model, airborne than a basic size kite of about 3 feet. It is still more difficult to fly a 12-inch or a 6-inch model, though they will fly well when made with care.

TOOLS FOR KITE-BUILDING   Very few tools are required for making a fine kite. A small saw (even a single hacksaw blade), a drill with a very small bit or, easier to find, a small gimlet or ice pick, a good pocketknife, a pair of scissors, and a sewing needle and thread are the only tools required.

MATERIALS FOR COVERS   You will need some strong, lightweight paper of various kinds, bought or homemade paste, some strong, lightweight string for stringing the kite, and some household or airplane glue. Many chain stores sell various sorts of paper suitable for kite-making, and one may find especially good paper for covering kites in a hobby shop or Japanese store. Ordinary tissue paper; thin, tough-woven, lightweight cloth, and thin plastic or cellophane may also be used for covering a kite, especially a larger one. Sometimes hard-to-find but good cover material is French or Japanese tissue paper.

WOOD FOR KITE STICKS   Strong, lightweight materials are best for building any sort of kite. When one decides to build a Malay, bow, or butterfly-type kite, the sticks must be made from flexible wood. It might be imagined that very lightweight lengths of bamboo or split bamboo strips would be best to assure flexibility, but bamboo has a few drawbacks. The chief one is that even when first soaked in hot water, bamboo, as a rule, does not bend easily enough to make a satisfactory bow for a kite. It is also difficult to find lengths of the same weight throughout. Short lengths, between knots, can be thicker in places or at one end. This throws the kite off balance so that it flies poorly if at all. This does not mean that light lengths of bamboo should not be used, since bamboo is a suitable wood for kite-building if well chosen. A very fine wood for kite-making is cypress, straight-grained and well-seasoned. All wood used for kite sticks should be straight-grained. Convenient sizes for the upright and crosspieces, given in inches, are: 36 x 3/8 x 3/16, 48 x 1/2 x 1/4, and 60 x 3/4 x 3/8. Pine and spruce are light, fairly strong, and good for larger kites. Old Venetian blind slats, sawn to the required sizes, or even well-sandpapered slats of a fruit crate, cut to size, make suitable kite sticks.

Sticks of the same weight and balance are needed, and if one end of a stick is heavier than the other, it should be sandpapered until exact balance is assured. After the exact center of a kite stick has been marked, it can be balanced on the blade of a table knife, to be certain that each end weighs exactly the same.

Balsawood is good, feather-weight material for smaller kite sticks. It can be cut very easily but it lacks strength, and is unsuitable for larger kites. Rattan can also be used, in some cases, where there is little or no strain on it, as in kites in fancy forms.

FRAMING A KITE   Framing, also known as stringing, is putting a string frame around a kite, to give form to the outside edges. The string should be of hard, twisted cotton with very little stretch to it. Nylon string is strong but it does stretch, so that the kite cover is likely to sag and lose shape. The string may be attached to the end of each stick by a secure knot, such

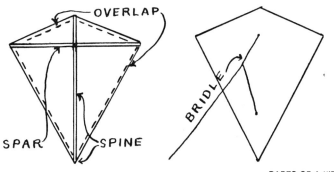

PARTS OF A KITE

Left: back view. *Right:* front view.

as the clove hitch (see Chapter 5), and tightened firmly but gently around and between each stick before going on to the next. Brushing over the framework string with shellac or glue adds much strength and firmness.

Another fine way, one of the best, when one has some skill in handling tools, is to drill very small holes at the end of each stick, thread the framing twine through the top of the spine hole first, then bring one end of the twine through each cross stick, knotting the string at the bottom hole, leaving a small loop or enough twine to attach the tail. This method is fine for plastic or paper covers but is not generally recommended for cloth covers, when the framing cord is best threaded through a narrow hem running around the cover.

CUTTING AND PASTING KITE COVERS A cover should be cut so that it is about 1 1/2 to 2 inches beyond the string of the frame, all around. Some kite makers cut this overlap into "V's" all around, about every two inches. This is necessary chiefly when cutting a cover to fit over curved sticks, as in Malay kites, to keep the cover from creasing. The overlap is made fast all around with a good paste, or liquid cement or glue. When the cover is made of plastic or cellophane, however, the overlap should be doubled, so that there are two thicknesses to fold over the string and fasten to the back of the kite with

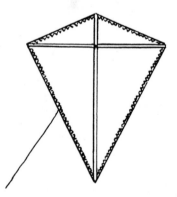

NOTCHED OVERLAP

cellophane or similar tape. Care must be taken not to stretch cellophane and plastic covers too tightly. Flat and box kites fly best with taut covers, while bow kites fly best with slightly loose covers.

A fine, if somewhat expensive, cover can be made of silk of almost any color, but white silk looks quite showy on a bright day and shows up splendidly after dark.

Covers should be reinforced where the bridle strings (see below) go through by pasting small circular patches of the cover material over these points. Patch any rents quickly, especially in plastic or cellophane covers, since the rents become enlarged quickly.

COVER DECORATION   When the kite cover is made of paper, white paper for instance, it may be painted with water colors or poster paints. Paint very lightly, with a big brush, so that it will not make a hole in the paper. The paper cover will sag but will become taut again as the paint dries. The cover may be painted with geometrical or wavy lines or decorated with pictures of birds or animals or some other design. Whatever is painted on a kite cover should be big, because the kite will usually be seen from a distance. A simple design may be drawn on the kite, covered with a light coat of paste, then sprinkled with glitter grains or powder. This makes the kite shine and sparkle, reflecting brilliant rays of light in the sunlight. Be sure that whatever decoration you use adds very little to the weight of the kite. In some countries, a lightweight brightly colored tassel is tied to the two parallel corners of diamond-shaped kites, and fighting kites often have the same decoration.

BRIDLE STRINGS   These are strings of various lengths from which kites are flown. The string or strings, attached to the kite sticks, come through small holes made in the cover, perhaps with an ice pick, and are fastened onto a lightweight plastic or other ring to which the string which is used to fly the kite is also attached. Instead of four separate strings, in a four-string bridle, two strings may be crossed and a lightweight ring fastened to where these two loose strings cross.

Much of a kite's performance is based on small changes in bridle adjustment.

ATTACHMENT RINGS A small, lightweight metal or plastic ring is very useful to attach to the bridle line, so that the kite-flying line may be looped onto the bridle ring easily, without having to tie a knot. Such rings are also fine for attaching additional kites to the main flying line. The rings take much of the knot breaking strain from the line, and attachments can be attached in seconds.

KITE TAILS For the millions of kites which soar and sway in the skies, tails are of major importance. A tail serves not only to steady a kite but also helps it to face in the right direction. Without tails, many kites could never become airborne. If a tail should drop off a kite which is aloft, the kite would dive or flutter to the ground. Tails supply the wind drag which balances flat kites and makes it possible for them to perform aloft.

If a kite bobs up and down, its tail needs to be shortened. When the tail is too short, the kite may dart about in the air but it will still stay up, in many cases, when flown cleverly.

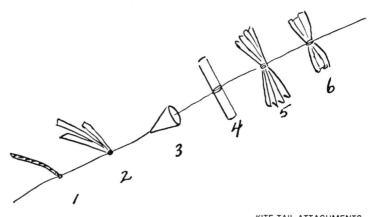

KITE TAIL ATTACHMENTS
(1) Rope. (2) Rag or paper strips. (3) Paper cup. (4) Folded paper. (5) Tissue paper "bow." (6) Rag "bow."

How long should the tail of a kite be in order to balance the kite in its flight? The kite's tail should be five times the length of its spine, which is the main vertical stick in the kite frame. This is not always exact, because the length can depend on the sort of tail used and, often, its weight. The length of tail necessary may best be discovered by amateur kitefliers by the trial-and-error method. A kite should be flown with a lot of tail to start with and shortened, bit by bit, until it handles perfectly.

Note the different kite tail attachments shown in the drawing and make the sort you like best, or different sets so that you can vary the kite-flying pattern. Some of the attachments are made of strips of lightweight paper, folded like a concertina. Cone-shaped paper drinking cups of various sizes make fine stabilizing attachments, as do paper strips or rags, cut streamer-fashion, as shown. Even a length of medium-weight rope makes a good tail strip in an emergency. The folded paper strips, cone-shaped paper cups, and other attachments are fastened to the tail, anywhere from 3 to 6 inches apart.

The folded paper strips may be from 4 to 6 inches long and about the same width. They can be folded either like a con-certina (pleated) to form a sort of bow tie, or folded onto them-selves, to form a solid flat tail. The size of the tail strips, the weight of the paper used to make them, and the number of folds in each strip, depend on the size of the kite to be flown. These tail strips are fastened onto the string tail 3 to 6 inches apart with a clove hitch or the simple form of lark's-head loop shown in the drawing under Knots for Kitefliers in this chapter. These make it easy to put on tail strips and remove them. Whether the tail strips are made of paper or cloth, the hitch should be made exactly in the middle of each strip, in order to look well and assure better balance.

Probably the best way to attach paper cups to a kite's tail is to make a very small hole in the point of each cup, either by using an ice pick or snipping a very small piece from the end. The kite tail string is threaded through these holes so that the pointed ends of the cups are downward, as illustrated. The cups are held in place by a big knot tied in the string under each point. (Tying on the cups so that the ends point upward

produces an entirely different effect on the kite's flight. It is interesting to experiment with this.) These tails look very handsome when the kite is in the air. The cups may be painted different colors, and kitefliers should experiment with different size cups in order to see which they like best.

Never tie a fishing sinker or a heavy metal ring to the end of the kite tail string to get balance. This is a dangerous practice which can cause a nasty injury either to the kiteflier, or, worse still, to an onlooker.

Lines

The line on which a kite is flown is also called cord, flying cord, or string, the popular name. Though kites may also be flown on fine, strong, lightweight wire, for scientific purposes, such a line should never be used for everyday kite-flying.

To send kites to the greatest height possible, the lines should be as lightweight and as strong as possible. Knots, especially "granny" knots, tied in any flying line, weaken the line. An old but strong, or a new nylon fishing line makes an excellent line.

A line of 25-pound breaking strength will fly a 3-foot up to a 6 foot kite, and larger ones too, in almost any normal wind. A 10-pound line will fly almost any small kite. Five-ply cotton string—the kind used to tie parcels—will fly medium-size kites, and smaller kites may be flown on strong nylon thread, sometimes called tailors' button thread.

Skill in kite-flying allows a kite to be flown on a very light line. Some young kitefliers have experimented with the use of lightweight crochet thread for flying fairly big kites. There is a chance of losing the kite, when using such a flying line, but there is challenge and the fun of "playing" the kite so that it doesn't break the line. The sensation is much the same as that of a fisherman who is playing a 25-pound salmon on a 6-pound test line.

The twine used for making fishing nets (seine twine) is excellent for kite-flying. Number 6, with a breaking point of about 12 pounds, is good for smaller kites. Other strengths are suitable for larger kites. Number 9, for instance, has a breaking point of 18 pounds. Seine twine comes in coils ranging from about 1,000 to 3,000 feet.

The experienced kiteflier's secret is the fact that he uses every effort to avoid a taut line between himself and the kite. A good curve in the line indicates that the kite is safe, no matter how high it has climbed or how hard the wind blows.

Man-lifting kites with a surface of 150 square feet of sailcloth and gear require anything from ¼-inch sash cord to ½-inch clothesline. For the 600-pound Japanese and Chinese kites with a surface of 800 square feet, which several hundred men and much ground ballast control, stoutly woven ropes 1½ inches in diameter, or even thicker, are used.

RESISTANCE TO WIND PULL Wind moves parallel to the ground and carries the kite with it. The pull of wind on the line and on the tail holds the kite at an angle of approximately 45 degrees.

The kite string should be able to resist the pull of the wind at the time the kite is being flown. For that reason, it should be twice as strong as the wind's estimated pull. Some experienced kitefliers never use a string of less than three or four times the estimated pull. They estimate the pull before a kite-flying session by using a spring scale when the kite is flying low soon after launching. To estimate wind pull, when a kite is flying in a fairly strong wind, hitch the kite-flying line to the hook at the end of the spring scale, while holding the ring or other attachment at the top of the scale. The scale will then register the wind pull in pounds. Estimating wind pull helps but, of course, as the kite rises it encounters different wind and gust conditions. The kite and string must be able to resist these conditions—often coupled with inexpert flying—or away the kite goes. Playing a kite skillfully helps an expert to use a much lighter string than would be needed by the average kiteflier.

Reels

Every kiteflier should make one or two reels or buy one if necessary. They are very handy gadgets and make letting out and reeling in line a pleasure. A big spool of almost any sort,

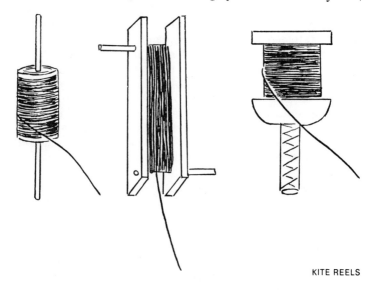

KITE REELS

with a dowel stick running through it, can be used as an improvised reel. A boy who is handy with tools can build this spool into a square or an oblong wooden frame. A reel can also be made from an old ping-pong paddle by cutting the bat into a square or an oblong, around which the kite line is wound with the help of the handle of the bat. An even simpler "reel" can be made by merely using an 8-inch length of 3/4- or 1-inch dowel and reeling the line onto that.

Types of Kites

There are dozens of distinct shapes of kites, many of which have been made by boys at home and flown successfully. Kites can be shaped like clowns, birds, butterflies, beasts, bats, boats, fish, frogs, dragons, and windmills. In all of them, lightweight material and balance are necessary. After building a few basic forms of kites, it is not too difficult to advance to the making of more complicated ones, though some box kites and compound, complex, kites are not easy to build so that they will surely fly.

There are actually three main types of kites: the flat, single-surface kite; the bow kite, and the box kite. They may all be built with variations which add to their flying qualities and/or appearance. Usually flat kites require tails of some sort; most bow kites do not, and box-type kites, which fly with one edge leading into the wind, never require a tail.

In the drawings on these pages, where the back of a kite is shown, the solid lines indicate kite sticks and the broken lines indicate framing string.

DIAMOND-SHAPED (BASIC) KITE   This kite is often called the two-stick kite, but that name is misleading, since a number of kites can be made with two sticks. The diamond-shaped kite, which is the most popular type, is also known as a single-pyramid kite. It is generally built with two sticks of the same length, or the vertical stick, called the spine, may be a little longer than the cross stick, known as the spar. This kite is flown with a tail, often five times the length of the spine, depending on the sort of tail used. Though this kite performs

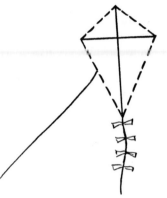

DIAMOND-SHAPED KITE

better when flown with a bridle, it may also be flown with the line attached directly to the point where the two sticks, vertical and horizontal, cross. In this kite, as in others of the same type, the spar should be glued on *top* of the spine, that is, on the side on which the cover is placed. Both sticks are then lashed securely together, to give the join additional strength. (See Diagonal Lashing, under Knots for Kitefliers.)

SQUARE KITE   The drawing shows how this kite is put together, by using two crosspieces of equal length, glued and

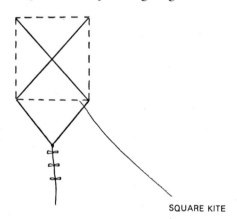

SQUARE KITE

firmly lashed, and tightly stringing the kite. The tail hangs from the center of a loop of string, slung beneath the kite, as shown in the drawing.

HEXAGONAL KITE   A kite of this shape may be made by using the stick framework of the square kite, described above, with a central stick added. However, there must be the same distance between the ends of the sticks, as indicated by points A, B, C, D, E, and F in the drawing. These sticks have to be

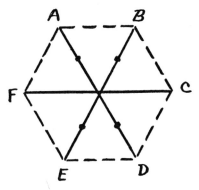

HEXAGONAL KITE

strung tightly by the framing string in order to give the hexagonal shape to the kite. The bridle should be attached to the upright cross sticks at the four points indicated by dots in the drawing.

BOW-TOP KITE   Instead of the straight cross stick, this bow-type kite is made with a flexible stick which is glued and bound to the top of the spine stick. Usually the top stick, forming the bow, has to be soaked in hot water or steamed in order to make it sufficiently flexible to be bent easily. The framing string is fastened to the end of one arm of the bow, brought down under the end of the spine, which should have a slight notch in it to hold the string, then on up to the end of the other arm of the bow, onto the end of which it is tightly tied.

GO FLY A KITE! • 123

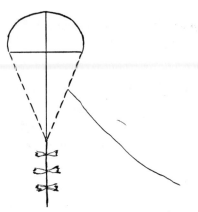

Of course, there must be tension kept on the string when stringing, so that the string frame will be taut and the cover nicely stretched. A four-legged bridle is used with this kite, one end of the string being attached to the end of each stick.

MALAY KITE This kite, sometimes referred to as the Malay-Eddy kite, is one of the finest tailless kites. It is not only a fine flying kite but also a formidable fighting kite, when

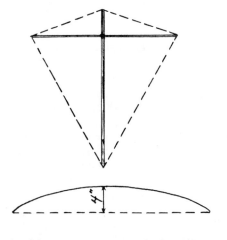

MALAY KITE

equipped for that purpose. It is a two-stick job but the top stick is bent like a bow, which so stabilizes the kite that no tail is needed. It is not difficult to make but the balance must be near perfect or it will have to be flown with a short tail, which any good Malay-type kite resents.

To make a Malay kite, cross two 36-inch sticks, spine and spar, in the form of a "T," with the spar about 8 inches below the top of the spine. A loop of strong string or a small, strong

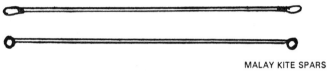

MALAY KITE SPARS
Top: spar with string loops. *Bottom:* spar with rings.

ring is bound onto each end of the spar. Now pass a strong piece of string (not nylon) through the two loops or rings and pull the string taut, so that a backward curved bow is formed which measures about 4 inches between the center of the bow and the tensed string. The bow can also be made by notching both ends of the spar, as in the drawing, and fitting a length of string, with a loop on each end, so that one loop fits into the notch at each end of the spar and is held in place by tension. Several tries may be necessary in order to have the string and loops the right length to fit securely into the notches and form a bow 3 1/2 to 4

TWO WAYS OF ATTACHING STRING TO MALAY KITE SPAR
Left: by notching. *Right:* by screw eye.

inches deep at the center. Another fine way to make the bow is to securely tie a small screw eye, with as long a shank as possible, onto each end of the spar. A length of string is then threaded through the two screw eyes, tensed, and tied to bend the spar into shape.

The kite is now framed with strong, lightweight string and a cover of strong paper or, better still, cloth is pasted or cemented into position by the overlap of cover material. It should extend beyond the framing string about 2 inches or a little more, and little "V's" should be cut about 2 inches apart, in the cover, at each end of the bow. The framing string should not be pulled too taut, or it may affect the curve of the bow. Even if the cover of this kite sags a little, it will not make this type of kite fly less well.

The Malay may be flown on a bridle of four strings of equal length, one attached to each corner of the kite and connected to a small, lightweight ring to which the kite line is attached.

Another form of this kite is made with the bow bent forward instead of backward. It does not fly quite as well as the above, back-bowed model, but it too is worth building.

FIGHTING KITES The Malay bow-type fighting kite is famous for its erratic flight. It is a two-stick job also, but the bowed cross stick is longer than the spine stick. This fighter kite is flown on a glazed, armored fighting line, beginning at the bridle and extending downward about 130 to 190 feet. Here, the regular kite line begins, being fastened to the fighting line by a knot such as the sheet bend (see Chapter 5). The fighting line is first coated with a very sticky gum and then dipped into powdered glass which cuts like a sharp knife when the gum hardens. The kite itself is armed with bamboo knives, while another bamboo knife is attached to the end of the tail. The owners of these kites duel from about 50 feet apart, taking up positions when the kites are aloft. Each combattant maneuvers his kite so that it cuts the line of his opponent's kite or wrecks it, in which case it becomes the winner's trophy.

BOX KITES This type of kite, and its variations, open up the three-dimensional world to kitefliers. These kites are difficult for most amateur kite-builders to make, but once a well-balanced model is built it flies very well and has a lot of lifting power. The details and general description given here, along with the drawings, should make it possible for even a beginner to make a box kite which will fly.

The four longer sticks, preferably of pine or spruce, can be

30 inches long by 1/4 inch or 3/8 inch wide, and the same thickness. The four short cross sticks, which are braces to hold the upright sticks apart, can be 17 1/2 inches long, 3/8 inch wide, and 1/8 inch or 1/4 inch thick. Each cross stick should have a small "V"-shaped notch cut into each end, as illustrated, so that they fit onto the upright sticks. To hold the kite together and provide the necessary wind resistance to make it fly, two strips or bands of strong, lightweight paper or cloth are needed. Each of these strips should be from 12 to 14 inches wide and 50 inches long. Each strip should be folded over about 1 1/2 inches at both top and bottom and the overlaps pasted down, or if cloth, sewn, to reinforce them. The two ends of each strip should be overlapped 2 inches and pasted or sewn securely together, after carefully marking the positions in which the upright kite sticks are glued, inside the strip, as follows: Four straight lines, each 12 inches apart, are marked with a pencil from top to bottom of each band, starting 2 inches from each end to allow for the overlap used for joining the two ends of each band. The kite is now ready to assemble.

Glue or cement the ends of the long sticks inside the bands, on the lines marked, leaving about 1/2 inch of the sticks showing at the top and bottom. Allow the glue to dry thoroughly

BOX KITE

Left: notched brace stick. *Right:* completed kite.

before beginning to assemble the kite. Now ease the two short sticks into each end of the kite, crossing each other in the center to form the square ends of the kite. Gently push these brace sticks down to about 4 inches from top and bottom of the kite, the notches fitting into the long sticks with the pressure of the brace sticks holding the upright sticks apart. Before easing the short brace sticks into place, carefully check them for length so that none of them have to be forced strongly into place. Should one or more sticks be a little too long, it is easy to saw a piece from one end of the stick so that each stick assures a nice snug fit and all are of exactly the same length. A new notch is made in a brace stick when one end has been sawn off. These brace sticks bend slightly, as each end is slowly pushed down the upright sticks, so that each band is held taut in the form of an exact square. Each pair of cross sticks may be tied together, where they cross in the middle, with a short length of thin, strong twine, which braces these sticks even more securely.

The flying line should be securely fastened to any one of the four long sticks, about 1 inch below the band. Box kites fly with one edge leading into the wind, and no tail is required when the kite is well-balanced. Box kites fly steadily and at high altitudes when well built and well flown.

Box kites can also be built in a triangular shape. This form of kite also flies very well.

Knots for Kitefliers

Many of the knots described under Handy Fisherman's Knots in Chapter 5 are also useful to kitefliers. Among them is the sheet bend, used for attaching lines together, whether to lengthen line or attach kites in tandem or other formations. Another fisherman's knot often used by kitefliers is the clove hitch, used to fasten framing string to the ends of kite sticks. The clove hitch is also used to attach bow-tie tail strips, paper tail strips, and cloth tail strips to a kite. This hitch is a very secure tie which is not so easily undone as the overhand and lark's-head knots, described below and also used for attaching tail strips to kites. When using the clove hitch for this purpose, pull the paper or cloth strip through the two loops and pull taut. The end loop, sometimes called the overhand loop, also described and illustrated in the section on fisherman's knots, is used to fasten the kite line to the ring. Once the loop is made, pass it through the ring and over it.

Following are some other knots useful to kitefliers. They are all easy to learn.

BRIDLE RING LOOP   This is a very easy way to fasten the bridle to a ring, to which the kite line is also fastened. The drawing illustrates just how this loop is made. To tie, make a bight

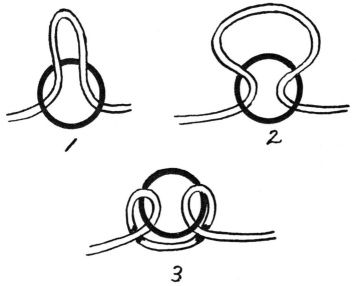

STEPS IN TYING THE BRIDLE RING LOOP

(bend) in the twine, as in step 1. Pass it through the ring, as in step 2. Then bring the twine ends through the bight, as shown in step 3. Pull taut.

TILLER HITCH   This is a boatman's knot which proves

very useful as another way of fastening a bridle to the line. Though perfectly secure when tightened, it may be undone as easily as a slip knot by a slight pull on the loose end, as indicated by the arrow in the drawing. To tie, make an end loop in the

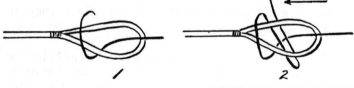

STEPS IN TYING THE TILLER HITCH

end of the bridle. Pass the end of the kite line down through the loop, up over and around it, as in step 1. Then make a bight near the end and bring it down between its own standing part and the loop, as in step 2. Pull taut.

If there is a ring on the bridle, follow the same procedure with the kite line as in steps 1 and 2. Pull taut.

OVERHAND KNOT   Encircle the paper or cloth tail strip with the string, and bring the end of the string around the standing part; then slip the end of the string through the bight on the other side. Pull taut.

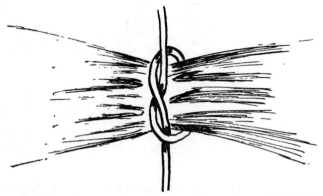

OVERHAND KNOT

LARK'S-HEAD LOOP   Make a bight in the string, as in step 1. Bring the bight down, to form two loops, as in step 2; then slip the strip of cloth or paper through them, as in step 3. Pull taut.

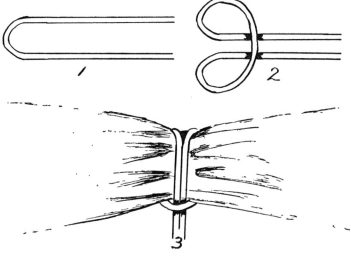

STEPS IN TYING THE LARK'S-HEAD LOOP

KNOTS FOR TANDEM KITE-FLYING   Flying two or more kites in tandem formation can be done most easily by attaching lightweight metal or plastic rings to the flying line at intervals of 10 to 20 feet. These rings are attached to the line by means of the bridle ring loop, described above.

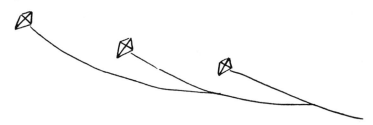

KITES IN TANDEM FORMATION

GO FLY A KITE! • 131

The flying line of the kite which is being flown tandem may be attached to the ring by a square knot or sheet bend, described under Handy Fisherman's Knots in Chapter 5.

DIAGONAL LASHING   This lashing is a good one to bind the kite spine and spar tightly together. Some experienced kite-makers glue these sticks together first, making the lashing right away, while the glue is still wet.

First, make a clove hitch around the spine above where the sticks cross. Pull the string or twine tight. Then make three or four turns of the string around one fork (where the sticks cross), pulling the string tight with each turn, to pull the two sticks as close together as possible. Make the same number of turns

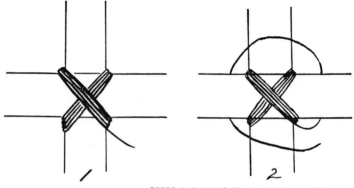

STEPS IN BINDING SPINE AND SPAR TOGETHER
Left: diagonal lashing. *Right:* frapping.

around the other fork, as in step 1, tightening the string at each turn. Now, make two or three frapping turns, as in step 2, to bind the turns which are holding the sticks together. Finish with a clove hitch around the stick nearest where the string end completed the frapping.

Kite-Flying Ways That Work

There is much more to flying a kite than simply getting it airborne and then letting out or reeling in line to keep the kite aloft. There are all sorts of tricks which will make a stubborn kite fly and even stunt once it is coaxed aloft. Even willing kites balk and dart from side to side in certain winds. Then it is necessary to see if the bridle needs adjusting, or whether the tail is too short or too long. A stalled kite can be sent higher by short tugs, known as "pumping" on the line, or brought lower by letting out some line fast. Should the kite begin to fall, it is getting too much line too fast.

Avoid too much sag or curve, called "belly," in your kite-flying line. A little sag is safe and will keep the line from snapping in tricky winds, but too much belly is a handicap. It was really pot-bellied sag that caused early kitefliers, trying for altitude, to fly kites in tandem and group formation.

If a kite darts when launching, let out line rapidly so that it grounds gently. Do not hesitate about reeling in a kite several times to make proper adjustments so that it will fly at its best. Even experts do this. Remember that you are not the only one who is doing the adjusting; the kite too is doing its share as it rests motionless in the breeze seeking perfect balance and self-adjustment. Practically every kite is different in its reactions to atmospheric conditions, and kites often react quite differently to different breeze and wind conditions. Get to know your kite thoroughly, and you can be among the champion kitefliers in your neighborhood.

With practice in line manipulation, a fellow can learn to make a kite fly to right or left, as well as up and down. The higher a kite flies, the more difficult it becomes to correct faulty flight, since the corrective tugs on the line take longer to reach the bridle.

LAUNCHING A KITE   The hardest part of kite-flying is to launch and land the kite safely. Launching a kite by running with it, though often seen, is the least recommended method. Often the kite or its tail catches and tears on some small projection on the ground. The only excuse for a running start is to cause the kite to rise into an area where there is enough lift to set it flying.

The nearness of buildings or trees in a park or other kite-flying area often makes it difficult to get the kite up and away, but real open spaces are scarce these days.

There are several ways to get a kite off the ground and into the air. The best way for practically all types of kites—small, medium, or even fairly large ones—is to launch the kite from the hand. Nearly all well-balanced kites appear to like this one-man, easy launching method. Simply hold the kite up gently by the towing ring with one hand, let out a little line, and the kite and the breeze will do the rest.

Another one-man launching method is used especially for flat kites. The kite is laid flat on the ground, with the top toward the flier and the tail stretched straight out on the ground behind it. The kiteflier stands a few yards back and pulls very gently on the line. As the kite tilts upward, it catches the breeze and should rise smoothly, pulling the whole length of the tail with it as it soars upward.

A helper who knows the ropes can be useful, under certain conditions, in launching. He should stand in front of and facing the kiteflier, at a distance ranging from about 60 to 90 feet. He holds the kite and when the breeze catches the kite, lets go gently, never tossing the kite into the air. The kiteflier helps the kite aloft by reeling in 20 feet or so of line.

Box kites should either be launched from the hand or sent up from the standing position. The kite should be stood with its rear end on the ground and its leading edge facing the wind. Step back a few paces and tilt the kite forward by pulling gently on the line. The kite should soar smoothly upward.

Bow (Malay-type) kites, too, rise willingly from the hand but may also be sent aloft by placing the kite flat, cover downward, on the ground. The curving front of this kite will catch enough breeze to lift it from the ground, whereupon the kiteflier exerts gentle pressure on his line, prior to letting out enough cord to send it on its way.

REELING IN A KITE   A well-made, well-balanced kite can be brought back to the hand when reeled in or pulled down. This, of course, is by far the best way to launch and retrieve a kite, since there is no wear and tear on it.

A good reel is a great help when bringing down a kite, since a boy may need over an hour to reel in a high-flying kite. The actual time required to reel in a kite depends on the size of the kite, the altitude at which it is flying, wind resistance, the efficiency of the reel, and how much the kite has to be played on its way down.

Warning: Kites should be reeled in with the reel held at nearly waist level, in order to protect the eyes and face in case the line snaps or a spool of line flies out forcibly from a wooden frame.

Tricks and Stunts for Kitefliers

There are many unusual tricks and stunts connected with kite-flying. Here are a few for kitefliers of all ages:

SENDING MESSENGERS Messengers are squares or circles of stiff or lightweight paper with a small hole pierced through the center and a slit cut from one side to the center, as illustrated. These messengers are slid onto the kite line from a

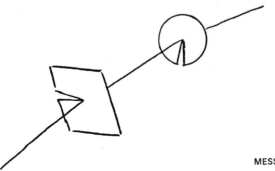

MESSENGERS

foot or two above the reel and, as the wind catches them, they glide smoothly up to the bridle of the kite. Often, they blow off the line at this point, and some kitefliers, when flying a kite high, take advantage of this by writing a little "Hi" sort of greeting on the messenger, followed by their name and address. The messengers often blow and glide long distances and, occasionally, cause a little note to be sent by their finders.

Another good type of messenger is the bracelet messenger, made from a stiff piece of paper 1 to 3 inches wide and from 6 to 10 inches long, with the two ends pasted or adhesive-taped

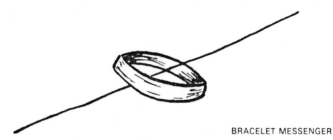

BRACELET MESSENGER

together. The second method allows the strip to be placed around the flying line in the field. When these rings are pasted together in advance, a reel used to hold the flying line may be too big to allow the rings to be threaded onto the line.

KITE-FLYING FROM A FISHING ROD   This is an interesting stunt which amuses fishermen. The kite-flying line is wound onto the fishing reel on a bait casting rod, and the kite is launched in one of the usual ways. Then the rod takes over, and the kite is played like a fish with only the reel and rod being used. Sometimes a kite is made to fly in an erratic manner, perhaps with a tail that is a little too short, which makes the kite difficult to fly. Some fishermen also fly such kites on a very lightweight line, for extra, sporting fun.

ILLUMINATED KITES   A small pencil-type flashlight can be securely fastened onto the end of the tail of a kite which is flown at night. To see a little light bobbing about in the dark, without any visible means of support, is mystifying. For variety, the bulb end of the flashlight may be covered with a piece of colored tissue paper or thin silk, held in place by an elastic band.

The same sort of flashlight as that mentioned above can be tied toward the foot of the spine of an ordinary kite. This creates a pretty effect when used on a kite, especially one covered with white, when flown in the dark.

"INVISIBLE" KITES AND TAILS   A kite covered with transparent or light bluish cellophane is nearly invisible, but will reflect light strikingly. When flown at a good height, the frame appears to float in the sky without a cover, but the tail is visible.

Tails which are practically invisible when the kite is aloft may be made from pieces of transparent cellophane, or translucent light blue cellophane. They can be made into cone shapes of varying sizes, depending on the size of the kite. Each cone is attached to the tail string, cone rim up, held in place by a knot on which the cone top rests. A tail of this sort matches well with the near-invisible kite, mentioned above.

TRICK BRIDLE ADJUSTMENTS   Shortening or lengthening the strings, or legs, of a bridle can greatly affect the flight of the kite. For instance, shortening the upper leg or legs of the bridle will turn a kite into a "floater," so that it flies almost flat. One must experiment with this shortened bridle stunt or the top of the kite may tilt so far forward and downward that it may dive groundward or jerk violently up and down.

NOISEMAKERS FOR KITES   Some boys like to have their kites make noises while they are in flight. There are a number of ways of doing this. Some attach a small, lightweight handbell to the tail of their kite, while others tie a small plastic whistle on top of the kite cover, lashing it to the spine.

One good way of making noise is to use an oriental type of noisemaker, called a hummer. To attach this to a diamond-shaped kite, the spine should be made 2 1/2 inches longer and the spar 5 inches longer than the actual edge of the kite cover. Another string is strung onto the kite frame sticks from the top of the spine to each end of the spar. (Some kitefliers lash short

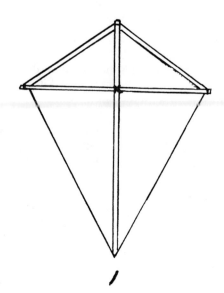

1

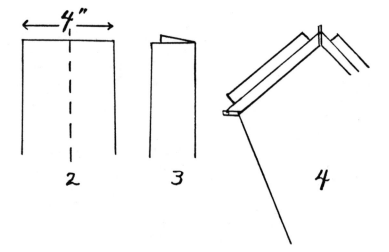

← 4" →

2 *3* *4*

STEPS IN MAKING A HUMMER

(1) Put extra string frame on kite from top of spine to ends of spar stick (2) and (3) Fold two strips of cover material lengthwise, as shown (4) Place strips of cover material over top string frame and paste edges together

lengths of sticks onto the ends of the actual frame sticks, so that they can be taken off when the hummer is not used.)

Two pieces of rather stiff paper, or cover material, about 4 inches wide, are cut so that they are long enough to reach from about 1 1/2 inches from the top of the spine to 1 1/2 inches from the end of the spar. These two strips are folded over the outer string, one on each side, between the top of the spine and spar, and pasted together along their entire length, half an inch from the edges, with the ends not pasted but left free so that the hummer may revolve freely around the string. These hummers flutter, turn, and make a humming noise when the kite is in flight.

On a square-type kite, the hummer, cut to the correct length, can be made exactly as described above, but only one strip is needed. It is attached to the hummer string, added to the top sticks of the kite.

Kite Contests and Tournaments

These contests may be held on a small scale, with only a few exhibitors and contestants, or as a big, spectator event. In certain months, when the weather is not too cool, the chance of rain appears small, and a stiff breeze or moderate wind is fairly certain, a few fellows may take a chance on organizing a kite rally, which can be a combined contest and tournament. However, handling such an event is often frustrating because, after three days of ideal kite-flying weather, on the fourth day— the day of the big event—it either blows a mild gale, is windless, or raining. Because of this, it is wise to hold some of the events listed below on any favorable occasion when a number of kite-fliers of all ages are in action. Good months for tournaments are late March and April, perhaps, though other months may prove equally suitable in certain areas.

In contests for older boys and adults, the weight of line used is sometimes standardized, to assure equal conditions for all contestants. Each kiteflier may be allowed a helper for certain events, as decided by the judges. To keep things moving, several events which do not conflict with each other may be conducted at the same time. All kites entered in competition must be able to fly.

Contests may be held for:

- the largest kite, which must be launched and flown successfully for five to fifteen minutes. First prize goes to the kite giving the best performance.
- the smallest kite which flies successfully.
- the best-constructed kite, judged by appearance, neatness, and strength.
- best design and decoration.
- the best all-around kite, with one event for homemade kites and another for bought kites.
- message-sending. A prize may be given for the most original messenger. Messages may be raced on, say, 100 yards of line, from the hand to the bridle. (One hundred yards may be marked on the line of one of the contesting kites, to give the judge an approximate distance.)
- Erratic flight. Kites are judged for their erratic performance—inspired by their fliers, of course—when flown at a certain height, say between 300 and 500 feet. Each flier uses winds to best advantage between these two heights.
- Launching and landing. The kiteflier wins who launches and lands his kite on a 300- to 600-foot flight in the smoothest and safest manner—"safest" meaning without any damage to the kite and, of course, the spectators!
- Altitude. Each contestant is allowed from 500 to 1,000 feet of line. A starting line is marked on the ground. The contestants begin to fly their kites from that line when a judge gives the starting signal, a whistle blast or the like. After a period of 6 to 10 minutes, a signal brings the contestants back to the starting line. The kite which is judged to be flying at the greatest height is judged the winner.
- Speed in unreeling and reeling. This event is for kites of the same type. Each contestant uses only 300 feet of kite line, and the contest begins and ends from directly behind a starting line. On a judge's signal, each flier launches his kite, lets it out to the full length of 300 feet of line, then reels it in as

speedily as possible. First kite in hand, with all line reeled in, is the winner.

With the above more or less standard practice contests for a start, you can probably devise other competitive events which will combine amusement with technique.

Safety Rules for Kitefliers

The following rules are suggested not only for the safety of kitefliers but also for that of other people who might easily be injured by a careless kiteflier.

- Obey all laws and rules regarding kite-flying in your area.
- Beware of all power lines, especially in damp or stormy weather, or if your kite line is damp.
- Never fly a kite in wet weather.
- Never fly a kite on a wire line unless an experienced kite-flying grownup is with you.
- Wear gloves when flying a kite of more than 4 feet, especially in windy weather. Kite pull on the line will burn or tear fingers and hands severely.
- Make certain that there are no low-flying aircraft in the area if you are flying a kite at over 1,000 feet altitude. A kite can cause an airplane crash.
- Take care of the birds. They cannot see nylon lines and often hit them while flying, killing themselves and snapping the kite line.
- When maneuvering a heavy kite at takeoff and landing, be certain that there is nobody in front of you. In such circumstances, a kite is a most dangerous weapon, whether yawing or diving to earth.
- Never fly kites in areas where there are a lot of people, especially on beaches, where winds are often tricky.
- Avoid flying kites across highways.
- Never try to recover kites caught on power lines, and better leave an entangled kite in a tree.

A boy should not fly a kite larger than 3 or perhaps 4 feet high by himself, and even then, the kite should not be flown in more than a light breeze or, for older boys, a gentle breeze, based on the mile-per-hour speeds shown on the Beaufort scale, explained in Chapter 7. Few boys fly kites successfully in a stiff breeze or wind greater than 14 miles per hour.

CHAPTER 9

Discovering Outdoor Games

THERE ARE NEARLY always some open, wooded spaces and play areas in large city parks, and quite often there are good play areas in smaller parks too. The sort of play areas available will decide just what games can best be played in the available spaces. Some activities can be carried out best on smooth, grassy ground, or asphalt or cement surfaces, while other games can be contested better on paths and in wooded areas. Here are some games which can be played on various sorts of terrain.

Wide-Area Games

Games of this sort can be played best by groups of four to eight boys, or more, though even two can play some of these games. The greater the number of players, the larger the play area should be, and a longer time limit can be set for such games. Time limits and boundaries are absolutely necessary in nearly all games in order to speed up the action, save players from wasting time out of bounds, and get the most out of the games.

RESCUE!   After choosing the section of the park in which this game will be played, establishing boundaries, and setting a time limit, the game can begin. The area used can be in the form of an oblong or square. It can measure 300 by 400 yards, more or considerably less, depending on the age and number of players and the size of the park. A fairly long pace equals one yard. Playing the game is easy.

On the border of the park or play area, an older boy is chosen to be the "lost" person, and he is given a start of about twenty minutes, depending on the size of the area and the time necessary for the lost person to get into it. The time when the hunt will begin is decided either by the lost person and the leader of the search party setting their watches so they agree on the time, or by the leader of the party blowing three blasts on a shrill whistle, to warn the lost player that the hunt is on.

It is impossible to set down any fixed, general rules for playing this game, because they must be decided chiefly by the area covered in the course of the game. For instance, the lost person may not be allowed to loiter in a building, since it is hard to find anyone in a big building, such as a park zoo. He may be instructed not to hide himself in a big crowd watching a baseball or football game, and the like. He may, however, take full advantage of wooded areas, hiding behind trees, logs, or brushpiles. This, when possible, turns the game into a real scouting activity, of the Daniel Boone type.

If time permits, after the first boy has been "found," a second lost person may be chosen and another search game played, or some of the other, shorter, limited-area games, given in this chapter, may be played.

PIRATE CHASE   A game, similar to the preceding one, is played in this way. The play area should be wooded, or dotted with clumps of bushes, when possible. After the area and time limit have been arranged, two boys are chosen, one to be the pirate captain and the other to be his first mate and guard. If the group of players is fairly large, say ten, for example, a second guard may be assigned to help the pirate captain. Before the game starts, players should be warned that they must not play rough, though the guards may hold a pursuer, if they can, for a minute or so, to protect their captain. The captain and his guard or guards should wear crepe paper armbands, about three inches wide, securely fastened on their left arms just above the elbows.

When the pirate captain and his helpers have been given the time set for finding concealment, the pursuers set out to capture the pirate. Only the pirate captain may be captured, and this is done by pulling off his armband. The guards will mislead the pursuers and interfere with their movements whenever possible, in order to help their captain avoid capture. The guards may not be captured, and their armbands are not snatched during the game. When the pirate captain's armband has been taken, the game ends.

The boys may decide among themselves to play this game in other ways. For instance, they may decide that the guard or guards may be captured also, by taking their armbands. A guard who loses his armband, in this version of the game, is out of the game and must take no further part in it. The players may also invent other rules, to meet conditions which arise during the course of the game.

FLAG RAID   To play this game well, it should be contested in a space at least 250 feet long by about 75 feet wide. Cover of some sort, such as bushes, trees, or rocks, helps to make this a more interesting game. There should be a group of at least six boys playing, equally divided into two teams. One boy on each team is chosen as its leader. Each team tries to creep up unexpectedly and grab the opposing team's flag.

This game is played best with a flag at each end of the raid area, one flag for each team. The flags may be pieces of cloth or paper, clearly displayed at the center of each end of the play area, and they may be hung on sticks stuck in the ground or tied onto low-hanging branches or bushes. Teams start from their own end of the raid area, and the game may be started by a leader blowing three shrill blasts on a whistle.

Each team works out its own strategy, in order to try to capture the opposing team's flag. This is not an easy job when there are only three or four players on each raiding team. If one or both teams decide on a flag guard, who is hard to spare from a small team, he can also take part in capturing, by tagging, any member of the attacking team. The guard must stand at least six paces away from the flag, unless he is actually chasing a raider who is trying to capture the flag. All players who are tagged must leave the game immediately.

To play this game really well, it should be carried out as a stalking and strategy game, players making good use of all cover when approaching a flag, and using various means, such as two players working toward the flag from different directions, in order to distract the guard's attention.

The least interesting way to play this game is to use a run, grab, and run method. When teams wish to play this form of the game, a flag may be set up in the center of the play area. In this version, each team, starting from a distance of about 100 feet, makes a rush for the flag when the signal is given.

KICKBALL RACE   This race is based on a popular one played by the American Indians. Individuals or teams of two to four Pueblo People or other Indian tribes kicked a buckskin-covered ball from 1 to 25 miles in these exciting races. The ball used ranged from about 2 1/2 to 4 1/2 inches in diameter, so for this game a soft rubber ball about 3 1/2 inches in diameter may be used. A hard rubber ball of the same size will serve, but it may be found a little hard on the feet. There is one ball for each team.

For the first few games, the race may be from a starting line, marked on the ground with string, tape, or paper cups. Kicking the ball all the way, players race to another line marked on the ground about 100 yards distant. Bigger boys may turn there and race back to the starting point. Playing like Indians, the ball must be touched only with either foot. A player who uses a hand to get the ball out of a hole is ruled out of the game.

For short distances, say from 50 to 150 yards, this game may be made more amusing by ruling that each player may kick the ball only with one foot. Of course, played on rough ground, this race becomes much more difficult, since getting the ball out of holes and hollows quickly, especially with one foot, is no easy job.

The team or Indian who finished any of these races first was announced the winner, and the same rule may be used in judging this game.

Games and Stunts on the Grass

Even when grassy ground looks flat, smooth, and free from small stones, it is wise to examine it carefully before playing games on it. All objects such as small stones, pieces of glass, and twigs should be carefully gathered up by the players and removed before playing their first game on that area.

TRIANGLE RACE   Two players may compete in this race, or it may be run as a relay, with two or three runners on each team. A triangle, with a base about 30 feet long, is marked on the ground by using 4 paper cups or 4 circles of cardboard or thick paper, each circle being about 8 inches in diameter. One

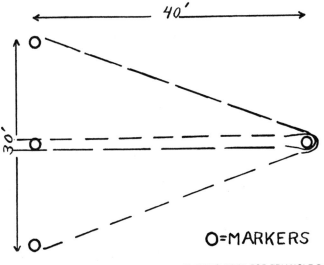

O=MARKERS

PLAYING AREA FOR TRIANGLE RACE

marker is placed at each end of the base of the triangle, and another marker is placed directly in the center of this base line, which is the start and finish line. The fourth marker is used to indicate the point of the triangle and is placed 40 feet away from and in line with the center base marker.

The players stand just beside the end markers, one player or team standing at each end of the base line. On the command, "Go," each runner runs to the triangle point marker, circles it, taking care not to collide with the other runner, and returns to the base starting line by running straight to the center marker on the base line. The first boy to finish wins.

In the team version, the first boy's arrival at the center base marker sets off the next, and so on, until runners have completed the race. The first team to finish wins.

WHICH-WAY RUN In this game, the players must be constantly on the alert in order to win. Small groups of three to ten boys can contest this activity.

The players stand just behind a line marked on the ground and face another line about 40 feet away, directly opposite them. One boy is chosen to lead the first game and he has a whistle which he should keep between his lips throughout the game. When he blows the whistle, the players must run toward the line opposite; then, on the second whistle they must stop immediately and run back toward the line from which they started. Each time the whistle blows, the players must turn and run in the opposite direction.

Runners who cross either line *after* the turn-around whistle signal are out of the race. The first player to cross either of the two lines *before* the turn-around signal is blown is the winner.

This game is as much one of wits as of speed. Though a runner must run fast, in order to be the first across a line before the turn-around signal is blown, he must have enough control to wheel quickly around, especially if he is very near the line when the turn-around signal is blown. Otherwise, he would cross the line just as or after the whistle blows and would be ruled out of the race.

The boy with the whistle must also be alert in order to keep the race going smoothly and at the same time trick some players into running themselves out of the game.

A different boy may do the whistling after each two games. The players will be able to judge which whistler gives them the most fun, and he may be asked to direct a few extra games. The boy with the whistle must use his head, so that the players do not run between the lines more than three or four times in each game, and he can rule out of the game any unsporting player who runs slowly between the lines, more or less marking time until the whistle blows again to signal the next turn-around.

It is the uncertainty in this game which makes it fun. The boy with the whistle may let the game end on the opposite line after only one run, from time to time, so that players do not slow down while awaiting the turn-around signal. It is to take runners by surprise that the boy with the whistle keeps it between his lips during the game. In this way, players do not know when a sudden blast is about to be given.

RABBIT HOP RACE   Two or more boys can contest this game, which will test their power of balance. They stand behind a line marked on the ground with string or cardboard, facing another line directly in front of them and about 30 feet away.

On the command, "Go," each boy places both hands flat on the ground, just ahead of him, with the arms straight and enough room between them for the legs to pass through easily. Immediately the hands are in position, both legs are advanced together, in a short hop, between the arms, and the feet placed squarely on the ground. Then the hands are pushed forward and advanced outside the feet and beyond them, and again placed flat on the ground. (If a contestant loses balance, he may be handicapped by moving back three or four feet.) Once again, the feet are advanced as before, and these movements are repeated as correctly and as quickly as possible, until the finish line is reached. The first boy to cross it is the winner. If decided in advance, the racing rabbits may turn at the second line and race back to the starting line, where the race ends.

This little game may be played also as a team relay, with two or more boys on each team. The contestants line up, one behind the other, behind the starting line, and when the first boy on the team returns to the starting line, the next in line continues the race. The first team to finish is the winner.

AROUND AND ON Two or more players can contest this little game at the same time, but one boy who does not play the first game or so should act as referee, in order to see that each player does the same thing as the others. Cone-shaped paper cups are placed in a straight line on the ground 10 feet apart,

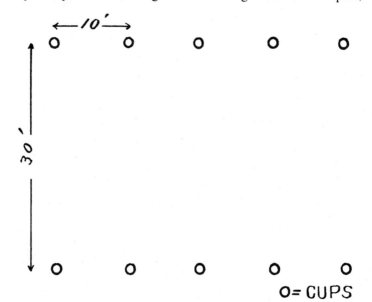

O= CUPS

PLAYING AREA FOR AROUND AND ON

with each cup facing another one, directly opposite and about 30 feet distant.

Each player stands behind a cup at one end of the play area. On the starting signal, each player starts circling his cup as close to it and as fast as he can, six times. Then he runs to the cup opposite, circles it six times in the same way, and races back to the starting point. The first player to finish, who has circled his two cups correctly, is the winner.

COME-ALONG TUG   For this stunt-game, two boys of about the same size and weight stand back to back on a marker or line. Directly in front of each player is another marker, about 15 feet distant.

The boys bend down and, stretching the arms between the legs, grasp each other's hands. Someone calls "Go," and each player, holding the stooping position, tries to drag his opponent over the line in front of him by pulling on his opponent's hands. If a player breaks the grip on purpose, he loses that tug, and the game begins again. The winner is the one who scores two wins out of three tugs.

THREE THROWS   This is a lazy sort of game, played while lying on the back in the grass. It may be played by one player at a time, or two players may contest the event. The player (or players) lies flat on his back and is given a big rubber ball, football, or volleyball. He makes the first throw by tossing the ball, with his hands, from about the waist, as high into the air as possible.

The second throw is made by trapping the ball between the ankles, raising the legs above the body to about the face, and then throwing the ball as far as possible, in the direction to which his feet pointed. Where the ball first strikes the ground is counted as the length of the throw.

The third and last throw is carried out with the ball held firmly between the ankles, as in the second throw, but this throw is made over the head, the ball traveling in the direction in which his head points, when the ball is released from between the ankles.

The game is not as easy to play well as it may appear from the play directions. The release of the ball at just the right moment from between the ankles, and the snap of the legs from the knees to send the ball as far as possible, are important in getting the maximum distance throws.

It is amusing to have both players, lying down about 8 feet apart, make the throws at the same moment. This can be done by a third player saying, "One, two, three, *throw!*" That boy can also decide which upward throw went highest, since the height to which the ball rises is a matter of judgment.

HEAVE! This is an amusing stunt-game which requires only a 12-foot length of fairly thick, soft rope, not less than half an inch in diameter. A pencil mark, ink mark, or piece of thin string should mark the exact center of the rope. Each of two players fastens one end of the rope around his waist. A bowline is best for this purpose. Then they back away from each other until the rope is taut.

On the starting signal, each player tries to pull on the rope, hand over hand, in an effort to pull the other player toward him. When they are within a foot of each other, the length of rope which each player has managed to pull in is measured, and the one who has taken in the longer amount of rope wins.

To tie the bowline needed for this stunt, pass the rope around the waist. Then make a small loop in the rope on your left, as

1

2

STEPS IN TYING THE BOWLINE

in step 1 of the drawing. Bring the end of the rope, at your right, up through the little loop, behind the long part of the rope, stretching between you and your opponent, and back down through the little loop, as in step 2. Pull the knot taut.

Tag Games

In most tag games, and many other games, plainly marked boundaries—or unmarked ones which are clearly understood by the players—will make it much easier to play in a sporting way. The size of the area should be smaller when only two to four play, and larger when ten or more are playing, but as a rule a circle ranging from about 100 to 150 feet in diameter will allow ample play space for the games which follow.

PASS TAG   In this game, the player who is It chases the player who is carrying a small ball, about the size of a tennis ball, or an 8-inch length of tightly rolled newspaper. The player escapes It by passing, not throwing, the ball or paper he is carrying to the player who is nearest him. This player must take the ball or paper, and then he is the one who is chased by It. The player who is tagged while carrying the ball or rolled paper becomes It, and another player is chased.

Players should keep moving throughout this game but must not run alongside, or rush in front of, the player who is being chased, so that the ball may be handed to them. The chased player gets rid of the ball when he is being hard pressed, but he should not try to pass it to another player when he is safely ahead of It.

KICKBALL TAG   In this novel form of tag, It tags a player by means of kicking a lightweight, big rubber ball—a volleyball will do—so that it hits one of the players, who becomes It. To start the game, the players stand in a circle about 20 feet in diameter, with It in the middle. He counts "one," and the players take off in different directions. When It counts up to ten, he dribbles the ball along the ground in front of him, while he chases a player. To tag that player, he must kick the ball so that it strikes the boy on a leg, but not above the knee. The player hit with the ball becomes It.

RUN-AROUND TAG   This is a really tough game of tag and is more fun with players who are fairly fast runners. After boundaries have been decided on, It counts up to ten and then sets off to tag a player. This player can escape being tagged by running completely around It. This is not quite as difficult as it sounds, because It must change the direction in which he is running, in order to tag the boy being chased. The circling should be attempted in a fairly small area and not by running directly away from It for, say, 30 feet or more. Of course, the closer the circling is done, the more sporting and amusing it is. Naturally, both the player being chased and It must be careful not to collide during the chase. When a player circles It, he is not chased any longer, and It sets out after another player.

NOT-AT-NOON TAG   This tag game is played in the same way as Japanese children play shadow tag. It is a tag game for a sunny or near-sunny day, since the player chosen to be It must step, or jump, onto the shadow of any other player, who then becomes It. This game is also a test of good sportsmanship, since It must feel certain that he has actually jumped onto a player's shadow before calling "It!" Also, the player, who may not feel sure that his shadow actually has been stepped on, should accept It's call which tells him that It has stepped on his shadow.

If the players feel that they are called "It" without cause—which may be so, in some cases—they may choose a player for the very difficult job of referee. He must be a good runner, because his job is to run close to It and make certain that the shadows of the various players really have been stepped on.

INDIAN HOOP TAG   This tag game is based on the American Indian game of hoop and lance. One Indian rolls a hoop, while another Indian runs after the hoop roller and tries to throw a lance through the moving hoop.

In this version of that game, a player propels a medium-sized wooden or metal hoop by a stick or by hand along the ground, while a second player tries to throw a fairly large rubber ball through the hoop. A basketball or volleyball is a good ball to use in this game. The players make a rule that even though a ball goes through the hoop, it does not count if the hoop is knocked over by the throw. When the thrower scores, he becomes the hoop roller, and the former hoop roller does the throwing.

Index